Stephanie Chukuruma

Taking
Christ as
Our Person
and
Living Him in
and for the
Church Life

The
Holy
Word
for
Morning
Revival

Watchman Nee
Witness Lee

Living Stream Ministry
Anaheim, CA • www.lsm.org

First Edition, April 2018.

ISBN 978-0-7363-9212-9

Published by

Living Stream Ministry
2431 W. La Palma Ave., Anaheim, CA 92801 U.S.A.
P. O. Box 2121, Anaheim, CA 92814 U.S.A.

Printed in the United States of America

18 19 20 / 4 3 2 1

International Training for Elders and
Responsible Ones—April 2018

TAKING CHRIST AS OUR PERSON
AND LIVING HIM
IN AND FOR THE CHURCH LIFE

Contents

Preface

1. This book is intended as an aid to believers in developing a daily time of morning revival with the Lord in His word. At the same time, it provides a limited review of the International Training for Elders and Responsible Ones held in Anaheim, California, on April 13-15, 2018. The general subject of the training was "Taking Christ as Our Person and Living Him in and for the Church Life." Through intimate contact with the Lord in His word, the believers can be constituted with life and truth and thereby equipped to prophesy in the meetings of the church unto the building up of the Body of Christ.

2. The book is divided into weeks. One training message is covered per week. Each week presents first the message outline, followed by six daily portions, a hymn, and then some space for writing. The message outline has been divided into days, corresponding to the six daily portions. Each daily portion covers certain points and begins with a section entitled "Morning Nourishment." This section contains selected verses and a short reading that can provide rich spiritual nourishment through intimate fellowship with the Lord. The "Morning Nourishment" is followed by a section entitled "Today's Reading," a longer portion of ministry related to the day's main points. Each day's portion concludes with a short list of references for further reading and some space for the saints to make notes concerning their spiritual inspiration, enlightenment, and enjoyment to serve as a reminder of what they have received of the Lord that day.

3. The space provided at the end of each week is for composing a short prophecy. This prophecy can be composed by considering all of our daily notes, the "harvest" of our inspirations during the week, and preparing a main point with some sub-points to be spoken in the church meetings for the organic building up of the Body of Christ.

4. Following the last week in this volume, we have provided reading schedules for both the Old and New Testaments in

the Recovery Version with footnotes. These schedules are arranged so that one can read through both the Old and New Testaments of the Recovery Version with footnotes in two years.

5. As a practical aid to the saints' feeding on the Word throughout the day, we have provided verse cards at the end of the volume, which correspond to each day's Scripture reading. These may be cut out and carried along as a source of spiritual enlightenment and nourishment in the saints' daily lives.

6. The content of this book is taken primarily from the published training outlines, the text and footnotes of the Recovery Version of the Bible, selections from the writings of Witness Lee and Watchman Nee, and *Hymns,* all of which are published by Living Stream Ministry.

7. The training message outlines were compiled by Living Stream Ministry from the writings of Witness Lee and Watchman Nee. The outlines, footnotes, and cross-references in the Recovery Version of the Bible are by Witness Lee. Unless otherwise noted, the references cited in this publication are by Witness Lee.

8. For the sake of space, references to *The Collected Works of Watchman Nee* and *The Collected Works of Witness Lee* are abbreviated to *CWWN* and *CWWL,* respectively.

International Training
for Elders and Responsible Ones
(April 2018)

General Subject:

Taking Christ as Our Person and Living Him in and for the Church Life

Experiencing the Central Work of God
and
Taking Christ as Our Person
in and for the Church Life

Scripture Reading: Eph. 3:16-21; Phil. 2:13; Gal. 2:20; 4:19

Day 1   **I. In and for the church life, we need to experience the central work of God (Eph. 3:17a; Phil. 2:13):**
  A. God's central work, His unique work, in the universe and throughout all the ages and generations is to work Himself in Christ into His chosen people, making Himself one with them (Gal. 4:19; Eph. 3:17a; 1 Cor. 6:17).
  B. God desires not mainly to do things for us but to work Himself into our being (Eph. 3:17a).
  C. God's intention is to have Christ thoroughly worked into our being; however, in our spiritual seeking we may have no concern about this, caring instead only for our intention (Phil. 2:21).
  D. God's purpose is to work Himself into us, making Himself our inward elements (Eph. 3:11, 16-19):
    1. This purpose is the center of the universe, and apart from this purpose the Christian life is meaningless (Rev. 4:11).
Day 2   2. The principle in God's work is to gain persons and by gaining them to have a way to go on:
      a. The proper priority is not for us to work for God but for God to work Himself into us (Eph. 2:10; Phil. 2:13).
      b. In the church life the importance of the person far exceeds that of the work (2 Tim. 2:20-22):
        (1) What we are is more important than what we do.
        (2) We cannot serve God beyond what we are as a person.

3. Spiritual progress consists in allowing God to gain ground within us (Col. 2:19; Eph. 3:17a).

Day 3   E. For the fulfillment of God's eternal economy, God needs to build Himself in Christ into our being, working Himself in Christ into us as our life, our nature, and our constitution, to make us God in life and in nature but not in the Godhead (2 Sam. 7:12-14a; Rom. 1:3-4; Eph. 3:17a; John 14:23; Col. 3:10-11):

1. We need God to build up Christ into our intrinsic constitution so that our entire being will be reconstituted with Christ (Eph. 3:17a).

2. Christ builds the church by coming into our spirit and spreading Himself from our spirit into our mind, emotion, and will to occupy our entire soul (Matt. 16:18; Eph. 3:17a).

F. We cooperate with God's central work by being poor in spirit (Matt. 5:3) and pure in heart (v. 8), seeking the Lord with a single heart (Psa. 27:4), turning to the Lord (2 Cor. 3:16), caring for the sense of life (Rom. 8:6), being willing to be enlightened (Eph. 1:17-18), and opening our whole being to the Lord to be filled with God as our content (3:16-19).

Day 4   **II. In and for the church life, we need to take Christ as our person (Gal. 2:20; Eph. 3:16-21):**

A. God's intention in His economy is to work Himself into us not only as our life but also as our person (Gal. 4:19).

B. Our regenerated spirit is the inner man with the indwelling Christ as its person (Eph. 3:17a):

1. If we would take Christ as our person, we must see that our regenerated spirit is no longer merely an organ for us to contact God but is our person.

2. In our inner man we have Christ not only as our life but also as our person (1 John 5:11-12; Col. 3:4; Eph. 3:17a).

Day 5

3. Our inner man consists of our renewed soul as its organ and our regenerated spirit indwelt by Christ, the person, as its life and person (Rom. 12:2; 8:10; Eph. 4:23; 2 Cor. 4:16).

4. We need to live in our spirit as the inner man by taking Christ as our person (Rom. 8:4; 1 Cor. 6:17; Gal. 2:20; Eph. 3:17a).

C. As regenerated believers, we have both the "I" (the self), our former person, and Christ, our new person (Gal. 2:20):

1. The "I" is in our soul, but Christ is in our spirit (Rom. 8:10; 2 Tim. 4:22).

2. The "I" is the person of the outer man, the old man, and Christ is the person of the inner man, the new man (2 Cor. 4:16).

3. The "I," the former person, has been crucified, and Christ, the new person, lives in us (Rom. 6:6; Gal. 2:20).

D. To take Christ as our person requires that we deny the self, our fallen person; we need to deny our soul-life and live by our new person, the indwelling Christ (Matt. 16:24-25; Col. 1:27).

E. In order to take Christ as our person, we need to deny our purpose, aim, and preference and take His purpose, aim, and preference (2 Cor. 5:14-15).

F. When we take Christ as our person and live not by ourselves but by Christ as the person, we become one with Him and no longer do anything according to our preference and taste but do everything according to His preference and taste (v. 15).

G. In order to have the church life, we need to be strengthened into our spirit as the inner man so that Christ, a living person, may make His home in our heart (Eph. 3:16-17a):

1. The inner man with Christ as its person is for our living in the church (2:21-22).

2. We need to take Christ not only as life in our spirit but also as the person in our heart (Col. 3:4; 1:27):

    a. When Christ makes His home in our heart, He becomes our person (Eph. 3:17a).

    b. The only way for Christ to be our person is for Him to make His home in our heart (v. 17a).

    c. If we take Christ as our person, allowing Him to spread into our heart, the person living in our heart will not be the self but Christ (Gal. 2:20).

H. If we take Christ as our person, we will live Him out as the proper church life (v. 20):

    1. Christ, who is our person, is for the church life (Matt. 16:18).

    2. Christ, a living person as our person, is the content of the church life (Gal. 1:1-2, 15-16; 4:19).

    3. It is not possible to have the church life when we allow our old man to be our person (Rom. 6:6; Gal. 2:20):

        a. If we want to live the church life but do not take Christ as our person, we cannot be blended with others.

        b. Unless we live by Christ as our person, we will remain natural persons, those who are according to their natural constitution, racial culture, national character, or religious background (Col. 1:27; 3:4, 10-11).

    4. The proper church life is a life in which we live in the inner man, taking Christ as our person (Eph. 3:17a; 2 Cor. 4:16).

    5. We should take Christ as our person and allow Christ to live in us and make His home in our heart so that we may be filled unto all the fullness of God in order to be the practical manifestation of the church as the Body of Christ (Gal. 2:20; Eph. 3:16-21).

Morning Nourishment

Phil. For it is God who operates in you both the willing
2:13 and the working for *His* good pleasure.
Gal. My children, with whom I travail again in birth
4:19 until Christ is formed in you.

God's economy is centered on one thing—God's unique work.
God's unique work in the universe and throughout all the ages
and generations is to work Himself in Christ into His chosen
people, making Himself one with them. This involves the mingling of divinity with humanity.

In order to work Himself into us, God became a man and
lived a human life on earth. Then He passed through death and
entered into resurrection and ascension, becoming the consummated, life-giving Spirit ready to come into us. When He
came into us, He regenerated our spirit. Now He is working in
us to increase Himself in us and to build Himself into us. (*Life-
study of 1 & 2 Samuel,* pp. 195-196)

Today's Reading

I have the burden to speak a word concerning God's intention to build Himself in Christ into us. God desires not mainly
to do things for us but to work Himself into our being.

Although there is no time element with God, nevertheless
He has, in the course of time, gradually, bit by bit, released His
revelation to man.

God is building Himself not in Himself but in man, and not
only *in* man but also *into* man. This building is God's constituting of Himself in Christ into man. (*Life-study of 1 & 2 Samuel,*
pp. 189, 205)

God's intention is to have Christ thoroughly worked into your
being, but in your spiritual seeking, you have no concern about this.
Your spiritual seeking is going in the opposite direction, only considering your intention....I am burdened that most of the saints in
the Lord's recovery do not see [this matter of God's intention].
(*CWWL, 1978,* vol. 2, "Life Messages, Volume 1," pp. 409-410)

God has no intention that you merely preach the gospel or

manage a church. God's intention is to work Himself into you through your preaching of the gospel and your managing of the church. His intention is to make Himself your inward elements.... By doing this, He kills two birds with one stone....He can accomplish the work, spread the gospel, and take care of the church through you. At the same time, through these works, He can have Himself added into you. God has no intention to correct your mistakes. His only intention is to work Himself into you and to fill you up, so that day by day...He would become ripened within you.

I hope that you will not take my words as a mere teaching. I am showing you something here. I am pointing out to you a way. I do not expect these words to give you some excitement or stimulation. I only hope that those who have a heart for the Lord would receive the blessing here.

If we read through the Old and the New Testament, we will see that God has one specific purpose in man. Whether in creating man or in redeeming man, God desires to achieve this purpose. This purpose can be considered the center of the universe. If a man does not meet this purpose while he lives on earth, he will feel empty. Even a Christian who does not see this purpose will feel that his life is meaningless. God has shown us in many ways through His word what this purpose is. God's purpose is to work Himself into man. At the end of Revelation we are told that in the new heaven and new earth, when God's work is completed, He will have worked Himself completely into man. By that time, God will be fully in man, and man will be fully in God. God and man will become one. We may think that we were destined for perdition and hell. After we are saved, we may think that now, as a saved person, we are satisfied as long as we can go to heaven. However, this is not the highest purpose of God, His ultimate purpose. God's highest purpose, His ultimate purpose, is to work Himself into man. (*Messages Given during the Resumption of Watchman Nee's Ministry,* vol. 1, pp. 122, 27)

Further Reading: Life-study of 1 & 2 Samuel, msgs. 26, 29-31

Enlightenment and inspiration: _____

_____
_____
_____

Morning Nourishment

Eph. For we are His masterpiece, created in Christ Jesus
2:10 for good works, which God prepared beforehand
     in order that we would walk in them.
2 Tim. If therefore anyone cleanses himself from these, he
2:21 will be a vessel unto honor, sanctified, useful to the
     master, prepared unto every good work.

In the church the most important thing is the person. The importance of the person far exceeds that of any work. In the world it is just the opposite; there, the work is more important than the person. But for us the person is more important. Time stands between the two eternities; both creation and redemption are within the span of time. During the span of time, God does many works. God's main goal, however, is not the works but to gain persons through the works. God does not work for the sake of working, but for the sake of gaining men through His works. God is not here merely to accomplish a work but to use His work to gain some people. Hence, our views have to be changed. (*Messages Given during the Resumption of Watchman Nee's Ministry,* vol. 1, p. 189)

Today's Reading

The service of the elders has to do with the person of the elder. It does not depend on the method but on the person. In the New Testament it is very difficult to find out what is the method or way to serve. Some places seem to speak about the method or the way, but actually the emphasis is still the person himself. The person is the way, and the person is the Lord's work. If God does not gain a person, He will have no work, and He will have no way. A way is a course that a person takes. If God does not gain man, He will have no course to take. Man thinks that the most important thing to do is to find a good way. However, God's work does not involve giving us the ways but is a matter of gaining the persons. If God can gain two or three brothers here, He will have a way. Even if I present to you the best way to be an elder, it will be useless if the person is wrong. We, the person, should be gained by God. We have to learn to be the proper person more than to learn to do the proper things. It is meaningless for things to be done properly without the person being a proper one. What you are is what you do. You cannot serve God beyond what you are as a person. Hudson Taylor said in his book *Union and Communion* that what we are is more important than what we do. This word left a deep impression on me. We should know how to help the brothers and sisters properly.

When the apostle spoke about the elders, he spoke very little about what they do. Mainly he spoke about the kind of persons they should be (1 Tim. 3:1-5).

If your heart is attracted by the Lord's love, you will be willing to give yourselves to the Lord. This is a very simple and direct word. The degree you can render others help is determined by the degree you have advanced yourself; it is also determined by the amount of learning you have picked up. If only one-fourth of those among us are used by God in this way, in a few years, the church will increase from one or two hundred people to one or two thousand, and the quality of the people gained will surpass the one or two hundred people that we have today. It is not our ground or our doctrines that will bring in God's blessing. The basic question is the person himself.

After a person is saved, all his spiritual experiences consist of allowing God to gain the proper ground within him. They consist of allowing God to live Himself out of him. Let me illustrate this in another way. Suppose there is an empty glass here. This depicts the condition of man before he is saved; he is empty within. After he is saved, he is filled within, in the same way that the glass would be filled with water. Do not say that salvation is to bring us into heaven. Salvation is to put God into us. The Lord washes us with His own blood for the purpose of putting Himself into us. (*Messages Given during the Resumption of Watchman Nee's Ministry,* vol. 1, pp. 59-60, 62, 29)

Further Reading: Messages Given during the Resumption of Watchman Nee's Ministry, vol. 1, chs. 4-5, 10

Enlightenment and inspiration: _____

_____

_____

_____

Morning Nourishment

John Jesus answered and said to him, If anyone loves
14:23 Me, he will keep My word, and My Father will love
him, and We will come to him and make an abode
with him.
Col. Where there cannot be Greek and Jew, circumcision
3:11 and uncircumcision, barbarian, Scythian, slave, free
man, but Christ is all and in all.

God makes us like Him by imparting His life and nature
into us. Second Peter 1:4 says that we have become "partakers
of the divine nature." John 1:12-13 says that we were born,
regenerated, by God with His life.

We have been born of God and today, having God's life and
nature, we are partially like Him. One day, when He comes, we
will be wholly and entirely like Him.

It was wonderful for David to be a man according to God's
heart, but it was not sufficient. God wants those who can say, "I
am not just a person according to God's heart. I am God in life
and in nature but not in His Godhead." On the one hand, the
New Testament reveals that the Godhead is unique and that
only God, who alone has the Godhead, should be worshipped.
On the other hand, the New Testament reveals that we, the
believers in Christ, have God's life and nature and that we are
becoming God in life and in nature but will never have His Godhead. (*Life-study of 1 & 2 Samuel,* p. 167)

Today's Reading

[In 2 Samuel 7] David wanted to build God a house of cedar,
but God wanted to build Himself in Christ into David. What God
would build into David would be both God's house and David's
house.

We need to realize that God will have a habitation not by
our doing or working but by His building. Christ builds the
church (Matt. 16:18) by coming into our spirit and spreading
Himself from our spirit into our mind, emotion, and will to
occupy our entire soul. This church will become His habitation

and our habitation. This is what we need, and our burden is to emphasize this one thing.

There is no need for us to build anything for God. Rather, God needs to build Himself in Christ into us as our life, nature, and essence. Eventually, the Triune God will become our intrinsic constitution. We will be constituted with the Triune God. That will be the seed of David and the Son of God—something divine and human satisfying God's need and our need for a mutual abode. The New Jerusalem is the consummation of this mutual abode, and we will all be there.

Second Samuel 7 is the unveiling of a prophecy through typology showing us there is no need for us to build something for God. We simply are not able to do this. We cannot build something for God with ourselves or with our knowledge of the Bible and theology. We need God to build up Christ into our intrinsic constitution so that our entire being will be reconstituted with Christ. As a result, we are not only changed, but we are transformed from one kind of person into another.

Perhaps now we can see that 2 Samuel 7 simply indicates that God does not need us to build anything for Him. We are nothing, we have nothing, and we can do nothing. Therefore, we need Christ to be wrought into our being.

At this point we need to consider once again what God's economy is. God's economy is to work Himself into us in Christ as His embodiment. Through death and resurrection Christ has become the life-giving Spirit (1 Cor. 15:45b). Now we need to let God work Christ as the Spirit into every part of our being. The more God does this, the more we will be able to declare, "To me, to live is Christ," and "I am crucified with Christ; and it is no longer I who live, but it is Christ who lives in me" (Phil. 1:21; Gal. 2:20). (*Life-study of 1 & 2 Samuel*, pp. 169, 160-161)

Further Reading: Life-study of 1 & 2 Samuel, msgs. 24, 28; Messages Given during the Resumption of Watchman Nee's Ministry, vol. 1, chs. 20, 22, 24

Enlightenment and inspiration: _____

_____

_____

_____

Morning Nourishment

Gal. I am crucified with Christ; and *it is* no longer I *who*
2:20 live, but *it is* Christ *who* lives in me; and the *life*
which I now live in the flesh I live in faith, the *faith*
of the Son of God, who loved me and gave Himself
up for me.
Col. When Christ our life is manifested, then you also
3:4 will be manifested with Him in glory.

The Lord's intention is to work Himself into us not only as
our life but also as our person. If we were just a box, and the
living Lord came into us to be our person, that would be easy. A
box has no person. But we are living boxes, and so many of us do
have a strong person. Some of us are strong in the mind, others
are strong in the emotion, and others are strong in the will.
Therefore, the Lord has some difficulty. But we must realize
that the Lord will never give up His own person. We must be the
ones who give up. The Lord has no intention of having us live as
a person. We should simply be the vessel that contains Him. But
the problem is that God created some living vessels. This is why
in the very beginning of the New Testament, the Lord Jesus said
that if we are going to follow Him, we must deny ourselves. This
means to deny our person. To follow Jesus means to take Him as
your person. (*CWWL, 1973-1974*, vol. 2, "The Wonderful Christ
in the Canon of the New Testament," p. 133)

Today's Reading

Every man is a soul with a body and a spirit as organs. The
soul is the person of every man. However, when a man believes
in the Lord and receives Him, the Lord becomes life to him in his
spirit. Before believing, man's spirit did not have life; it was
merely an organ. However, once the Lord Jesus enters into a
man's spirit as life, his spirit is no longer merely an organ but
also an inner man.

We must be clear concerning this matter. Formerly, our soul
was our person, but today our spirit is our person. Formerly, the
spirit was an organ, but now the soul is an organ. We should not

let our soul voice its opinions or take the lead. This is to deny the expression of our soul as our person. However, when we need to remember certain things, we can utilize the faculty of our mind as an organ related to memory. Thus, our soul is no longer our person but merely an organ. Our spirit is our person today. (*CWWL, 1970*, vol. 3, "Taking Christ as Our Person for the Church Life," pp. 488-490)

The outward man includes our body and our soul, with the body as its organ and the soul as its life and person. The inward man includes our regenerated spirit and our renewed soul with the regenerated spirit as its life and person and the renewed soul as its organ. The life of the soul must be denied (Matt. 16:24-25), but the functions of the soul, the mind, will, and emotion, must be renewed and uplifted by being subdued (2 Cor. 10:4-5) to be used by the spirit, which is the person of the inward man. (*Life-study of 2 Corinthians*, p. 306)

We now have two lives—the human life in our soul and the divine life in our spirit—and two men—the outer man, which is a soulish man, and the inner man, which is a spiritual man. We cannot live by these two lives simultaneously; we can live by only one life at a time. Therefore, we should live not by the human life but by the divine life, not by the outer man but by the inner man.

Long before we were born, our old man had been crucified with Christ (Rom. 6:6; Gal. 2:20). Hence, we should not live by the soulish man, the outer man, but by the spiritual man, the inner man. Second Corinthians 4:16 says, "Though our outer man is decaying, yet our inner man is being renewed day by day." Our outer man is being consumed and worn out by the killing work of death, but our inner man is being nourished with the fresh supply of the resurrection life. We need to live by the inner man, the new man, which has Christ as its life. To live by the inner man is to live by Christ as our person, because Christ is in the inner man as its life. (*CWWL, 1970*, vol. 2, pp. 495-496)

Further Reading: CWWL, 1970, vol. 2, pp. 337-341, 493-499

Enlightenment and inspiration: _____

_____

_____

_____

Morning Nourishment

2 Cor. Therefore we do not lose heart; but though our
4:16 outer man is decaying, yet our inner *man* is being
renewed day by day.

5:15 And He died for all that those who live may no
longer live to themselves but to Him who died for
them and has been raised.

Our regenerated human spirit is not only an organ to know
God's surpassingly great power but also the inner man with the
indwelling Christ as its person. We need to live in our spirit as
the inner man by taking Christ as our person. We should be
strengthened into our inner man so that Christ may make His
home in our heart, and we should take Christ not only as our life
and power but also as our person.

We need to take Christ as our person. Our former person, our
self, was in our soul, but our new person, Christ, is in our spirit.
Therefore, we need to deny our self, our old person, and take
Christ as our new person. In order to take Christ as our person,
we must put our self aside. (*CWWL, 1970*, vol. 2, p. 496)

Today's Reading

In our inner man, our regenerated spirit, we have Christ not
only as our life but also our person. In Galatians 2:20 Paul says, "I
am crucified with Christ; and it is no longer I who live, but it is
Christ who lives in me." As believers, we have both the "I" (the
self), our former person, and Christ, our new person. The "I" is in
our soul, but Christ is in our spirit. The "I" is the person of the
outer man, the old man, but Christ is the person of the inner man,
the new man. There are two persons within us: the "I" and Christ.
The "I," our former person, has been crucified (Rom. 6:6), and
Christ, our new person, lives in us. It is no longer "I" but Christ.

Many Christians know that Christ is our power and our life,
but few realize that He also is our person. Christ is not only the
reality of all the divine attributes but also the person of our
inner man. As regenerated believers we have Christ Himself
within us as our person. We lack the language, the utterance, to

explain this marvelous and profound mystery.

We need to see the difference between life and a person. Whereas life is the means by which we live, a person is a living being with a purpose, aim, choice, and preference. We should not only live by Christ as our life but also take Him as our person. In order to take Christ as our person, we need to deny our own purpose, aim, and preference and take His purpose, aim, and preference.

We need to take Christ as our person in our daily walk. If we intend to go to a department store to purchase certain items, our primary focus should not be whether what we purchase is of the Lord's will but who makes the purchase—the self or Christ.... When we are about to purchase a certain item, we should pray, "Lord, You are my person. Would You buy this?..." If we take Christ as our person in the practical matter of shopping, we will be able to declare with assurance, "It is not I who shop but Christ."

Christ, who is our person, is for the church life. We should allow Christ to live in us and make His home in our heart so that we may be filled unto all the fullness of God in order to be the practical manifestation of the church as the Body of Christ (Eph. 1:22-23; 3:19). We should live in the inner man by taking Christ as our person so that we may have a proper, living, and rich church life. If we live a daily life in which we take Christ as our person, we will come together in the meetings not only with Christ but also as the corporate Christ (1 Cor. 12:12). In such meetings we will render real worship to the Father, worshipping Him in our spirit and with Christ as the divine reality (John 4:24). May the Lord open our eyes to see that we need to be strengthened into our inner man so that Christ may make His home in our heart. If Christ takes full possession of our being, we will enjoy Him as everything in the church and will bring forth the practicality of the church as the new man, where Christ is all and in all (Col. 3:10-11). (*CWWL, 1970,* vol. 2, pp. 502-503, 498-499)

Further Reading: CWWL, 1970, vol. 2, pp. 501-516; *The Way to Build Up the Church* (booklet)

Enlightenment and inspiration: _____

_____

_____

_____

Morning Nourishment

Eph. **That Christ may make His home in your hearts**
3:17 through faith, that you, being rooted and grounded
in love.
21 To Him be the glory in the church and in Christ Jesus
unto all the generations forever and ever. Amen.

When Christ is in our spirit, He is our life, but when Christ spreads into our heart, He becomes our person. We need to take Christ not only as life in our spirit but also as the person in our heart.

If we take Christ as our person, allowing Him to spread into our heart, the person living in our heart will not be the self but Christ (Gal. 2:20). In a practical way our heart needs to become Christ's home. He must be able to live in us and to settle down in us. He, not the self, must be the One who occupies our heart. The crucial question is who is living in our heart and who is the person taking up residence in our heart. As long as we are still the person living in our heart, our heart is the home of the self, not the home of Christ. For this reason, we need to pray for ourselves and for others to have the reality of taking Christ as our person in our daily living. (*The Conclusion of the New Testament,* p. 3390)

Today's Reading

Everything we do should be done not by the self but by Christ. His tastes and preferences need to become ours. Then Christ will be not only our life but also our person. The Lord will thus expand in our heart, take possession of our heart, and make His home in our heart in a full way. Eventually, He will saturate our whole being with Himself, and we will live no longer by the self but by Christ. (*The Conclusion of the New Testament,* pp. 3390-3391)

If we want to live the church life but do not take Christ as our person, we can never be blended together with others, because we are all different according to our nature. Each of us has our own tastes and preferences. We may experience the resurrection power of Christ when we are by ourselves, but when we come to the meeting hall, our tastes and preferences can easily rise up within us. We may experience the resurrection power before coming to the meeting hall, but when we are asked to clean chairs in a specific way, we can easily be bothered....It is not possible to have the church life when our old man is allowed to be our person. Those who want to have the church life must deny their soul-life, their self, their old man. We should all cover our heads and take Christ as our person. (*CWWL, 1970,* vol. 3, "Taking Christ as Our Person for the Church Life," pp. 492-493)

Christ, a living person, is the content and reality of the church life. Unless we live by Christ as our person, we will remain natural persons, those who live according to their natural constitution, racial culture, national character, or religious background. However, if we take Christ as our person, He will make His home in our heart, spread within us, and take over our entire inner being. As a result, we will be constituted with Christ and thereby live in the church life in a practical way. (*CWWL, 1970,* vol. 2, p. 504)

The church today is the new man, and the person of this new man is Christ Himself. We all must take Him as our person. In His person we will have the church life.

We should not only know the church as the Body, but we should also take a further step and see the church as the new man and the Lord as the person of the new man. When we reach this point, we will be rooted and grounded in the Lord's love and able to apprehend with all the saints the breadth, the length, the height, and the depth of Christ (Eph. 3:17-18). At this time we will also know the sweetness of His love, which surpasses all knowledge, and be filled unto the fullness of God (v. 19). Thus, we put off the old man and put on the new man daily (4:22-24). This new man is the church life. (*CWWL, 1970,* vol. 3, "Taking Christ as Our Person for the Church Life," pp. 530-531)

Further Reading: CWWL, 1970, vol. 3, "Taking Christ as Our Person for the Church Life," chs. 4, 7, 10

Enlightenment and inspiration: _____

_____

_____

_____

Hymns, #1325

1 God eternal has a purpose,
Formed in His eternal past,
Spreading to eternal future;
'Twixt these ends all time is cast.
For with time there is the process,
Time for His accomplishment;
And in time we're merely travelers—
For eternity we're meant.

2 God would have a group of people
Built together in His plan,
Blended, knit, coordinated
As His vessel—one new man.
God would come into this vessel
With His nature, life, and ways,
Mingling Spirit with our spirits
For His joy and to His praise.

3 God has worked in three directions
For His plan so marvelous:
As the Father, Son, and Spirit
To dispense Himself to us!
All creation gives the setting—
Heav'n and earth are for this plan;
'Tis for this God made a body,
Soul, and spirit—three-part man.

4 As the center, as the kernel,
Of God's plan our spirit is;
Calling on the name of Jesus
Makes our spirit one with His.
From the center to circumf'rence
God would saturate each part;
Feeling, mind, and will renewing,
Making home in all our heart.

5 Thus in life we're built together,
Then in love we're knit as one;
God is now His plan fulfilling,
Finishing what He's begun.
Lord, increase Thyself within us
That we might be built by Thee
Into that great corporate vessel
Filled with God exclusively.

6   As the product, the fulfillment,
     Will the church in glory stand,
     Consummation of the purpose
     In eternal ages planned.
     God will have His corporate vessel,
     All His glory to contain;
     Lord, we're wholly for Thy purpose,
     All Thy goal in us attain.

Composition for prophecy with main point and sub-points: _____

_____
_____
_____
_____
_____
_____
_____
_____
_____
_____
_____
_____
_____
_____
_____
_____
_____
_____
_____
_____
_____
_____
_____
_____
_____
_____
_____
_____
_____
_____
_____

Becoming Pillars and Pillar Builders in and for the Building of God

Scripture Reading: Matt. 16:18; Gen. 28:10-22; Prov. 4:18; 1 Kings 7:17-20; Rev. 3:12

Day 1   **I. Jacob's dream unveils that God desires to have a house on earth, and His intention is to transform His called ones into stones, pillars, material for His building (Gen. 28:10-22; Matt. 16:18; 1 Pet. 2:4-5; Rev. 3:12):**

A. In the book of Genesis there are two kinds of pillars— the pillar of salt (19:26), which indicates shame, and the pillar of stone (28:18; 35:14), which indicates building in strength (1 Kings 7:21).

B. In Genesis 28 Jacob was a supplanter, but by the time we come to chapter 48, this supplanter has been thoroughly transformed into a man of God; this man of God is the pillar (28:18, 22a; cf. Prov. 4:18).

C. "He who overcomes, him I will make a pillar in the temple of My God, and he shall by no means go out anymore, and I will write upon him the name of My God and the name of the city of My God, the New Jerusalem, which descends out of heaven from My God, and My new name" (Rev. 3:12, cf. v. 8):

1. The word *make* is very significant, meaning to constitute into something, to construct in a creative way; the Lord makes us pillars by transforming us, that is, by carrying away our natural element and by replacing it with His divine essence (2 Cor. 3:18; Rom. 12:2).

Day 2   2. For the overcomers to be pillars in the temple means that they will be pillars in the Triune God, for the temple is "the Lord God the Almighty and the Lamb" (Rev. 21:22; cf. Psa. 90:1; John 14:23).

II. **The life and experience of Jacob reveal the way that we can be transformed into pillars for God's building:**

A. Since our selection was according to God's mercy, we need to continually depend on His mercy, enjoying His new mercies day by day to become vessels of mercy, honor, and glory (Rom. 9:11-13, 16, 21, 23; Lam. 3:21-24).

B. We need to enjoy Him as the All-sufficient God (Gen. 48:3; 17:1; Phil. 1:19).

C. We need to enjoy His continual shepherding until the end of our days—"the God who has shepherded me all my life to this day" (Gen. 48:15b; Rev. 3:8).

D. We need to behold God's face (Gen. 32:30; 2 Cor. 3:18; 4:6-7), seek His face (Psa. 27:8, 4), enjoy His face as our serving supply (Exo. 25:30; 33:11a), doing everything in the face, the person, of Christ for our transformation from glory to glory (2 Cor. 2:10; cf. 13:14); when the Triune God is dispensed into us, we have the face of the Triune God as our grace and His countenance as our peace (Num. 6:25-26):

1. Seeing God equals gaining God to be constituted with God (Job 42:5-7).

2. Seeing God transforms us because in seeing God, we receive His element into us, and our old element is discharged (2 Cor. 3:18; Rom. 12:2).

E. In the Scriptures the pillar is a sign, a testimony, of God's building through transformation in practicing the Body life (Gen. 28:22a; 1 Kings 7:15-22; Gal. 2:9; 1 Tim. 3:15; Rev. 3:12; Rom. 12:2; Eph. 4:11-12):

1. According to Genesis 28:18, Jacob took the stone that he had made his pillow and set it up for a pillar:

a. The stone becoming a pillow signifies that the divine element of Christ constituted into our being through our subjective experience of Him becomes a pillow for our rest (cf. Matt. 11:28).

Day 3   b. The pillow becoming a pillar signifies that the Christ whom we have experienced and on whom we rest becomes the material and the support for God's building, God's house (1 Kings 7:21; 1 Tim. 3:15).

2. The pillars of the temple were built of bronze, signifying God's judgment (1 Kings 7:14-15; cf. John 3:14):
    a. Those who are useful to God are constantly under God's judgment, realizing that they are men in the flesh, worthy of nothing but death and burial (Psa. 51:5; Exo. 4:1-9; Rom. 7:18; Matt. 3:16-17).
    b. We must judge ourselves as nothing and being only qualified to be crucified; whatever we are, we are by the grace of God, and it is not we who labor but the grace of God (1 Cor. 15:10; Gal. 2:20; 1 Pet. 5:5-7).

Day 4   c. The reason for both division and fruitlessness among believers is that there is no bronze, nothing of God's judgment; instead, there is pride, self-boasting, self-vindication, self-justification, self-approval, self-excuse, self-righteousness, condemning others, and regulating others instead of shepherding and seeking them (Matt. 16:24; Luke 9:54-55).

3. On the capitals of the pillars in the temple were "nets of checker work [like a trellis] with wreaths of chain work"; these signify the complicated and intermixed situation in which those who are pillars in God's building live and bear responsibility (1 Kings 7:17).

4. On the top of the capitals were lilies and pomegranates (vv. 18-20):

   a. Lilies signify a life of faith in God, a life of
      living by what God is to us, not by what
      we are; the bronze means "not I," and the
      lily means "but Christ" (S. S. 2:1-2; Matt.
      6:28, 30; cf. 2 Cor. 5:4; Gal. 2:20).
   b. The pomegranates on the wreaths of the
      capitals signify the fullness, the abun-
      dance and beauty, and the expression of
      the riches of Christ as life (1 Kings 7:20;
      cf. Phil. 1:19-21a).
   c. Through the crossing out of the network
      and the restriction of the chain work, we
      can live a pure, simple life of trusting in
      God to express the riches of the divine
      life of Christ for God's building in life.
 F. In spiritual significance the bowls of the capitals
    are a testimony (two) indicating that those who
    place themselves under God's judgment (bronze),
    counting themselves as nothing, are able to bear
    responsibility (five) in full (ten) and express the
    riches of the divine life (pomegranates) in the
    midst of a complicated and intermixed situation
    (the checker work and chain work) out of the
    process of resurrection (the base of the capitals,
    three cubits in height) because they do not live by
    themselves but by God (lilies).
III. **Solomon, the builder of the temple, is a type
     of Christ (Matt. 12:42), and Hiram, the builder
     of the pillars (1 Kings 7:13-15), is a type of the
     gifted persons in the New Testament, who
     perfect the saints for the building up of the
     Body of Christ (Eph. 4:8, 11-12, 16):**
   A. That the work of building was not done by Solo-
      mon directly but by Solomon through Hiram
      indicates that Christ builds up the church not
      directly but through the gifted persons.
   B. Second Chronicles 2:14 says that Hiram's mother
      was "a woman of the daughters of Dan"; the tribe
      of Dan is the tribe of idolatry that caused God's

people to stumble and fall from God's way (Gen. 49:17); the fact that Hiram's mother was of Dan indicates that Hiram's origin, like that of all men, was of sin (Psa. 51:5; cf. John 8:44a).

C. Hiram "was the son of a widow and of the tribe of Naphtali, and his father was a man of Tyre, a bronze worker; and he was full of wisdom and understanding and skill to do all kinds of work in bronze" (1 Kings 7:14):

1. That Hiram became one who was "of the tribe of Naphtali" (v. 14), the tribe of resurrection, that is, of transformation (Gen. 49:21), signifies that in order to be a part of God's building and participate in its building work, we need to be transferred from the "tribe of Dan" into the "tribe of Naphtali" by being regenerated and transformed in Christ's resurrection (1 Pet. 1:3; 2 Cor. 3:15-18).

Day 6

2. "Naphtali is a hind let loose; / He gives beautiful words" (Gen. 49:21):

a. A hind is a person who trusts and rejoices in God in a desperate situation (Hab. 3:17-18).

b. Habakkuk 3:19 says, "Jehovah the Lord is my strength; / And He makes my feet like hinds' feet / And will cause me to walk on my high places."

c. "The hind of the dawn" is also mentioned in the title of Psalm 22, which is on Christ in resurrection for the church (v. 22; Heb. 2:12; S. S. 2:8-9); Naphtali is a tribe of the hind, signifying a regenerated and transformed person who trusts in God, walks on the mountaintops, and lives in resurrection for the church life.

d. Naphtali was in the land of Galilee (Matt. 4:15), and the first group of apostles came from Galilee (Acts 1:11); the beautiful words that came out of these Galileans were the word of life (5:20), the word of grace (14:3), the word of salvation (13:26), the word of wisdom (1 Cor. 12:8), the word of knowledge (v. 8), and the word of building (Acts 20:32).

3. Tyre was a Gentile city noted for its commerce; hence, it was one with Satan (Ezek. 28:12, 16).

4. Hiram's father was the source of Hiram's skill in working with bronze; however, his father died, leaving his mother, the source of his existence, a widow:

   a. This signifies that in order to be useful to God for the building of the church, God's dwelling place, we need to acquire the secular learning and skills but must allow our "Tyrian" father, the source of these things, to die.

   b. Furthermore, our "Danite" mother must be "widowed" (separated from the worldly source), and we must be of the "tribe of Naphtali," the tribe of transformation.

   c. Thus, we continue to possess the learning and the skills without the source, our existence (mother) is no longer linked to our worldly origin, and we are in resurrection; Moses and the apostle Paul are excellent examples of this principle.

D. Hiram was brought from Tyre to King Solomon in Jerusalem (1 Kings 7:13-14), the place where the temple was to be built; Jerusalem typifies the church:

1. Both today's Solomon (Christ) and God's present building are in the church.

2. Thus, in order to be useful to God for His building, we must gain secular skills, live in resurrection, and come to the proper ground, the ground of the church (Rev. 1:10-11).

IV. The need in the church today is for the Lord to

gain pillars and pillar builders; in order for
this need to be met, we all must pray to the
Lord, saying, "Lord, for the sake of Your building, make me a pillar and a pillar builder."

we must first become pillars ourselves
in order to be those who produce
pillars.

Morning Nourishment

Gen. And Jacob rose up early in the morning and took
28:18 the stone that he had put under his head, and he
set it up as a pillar and poured oil on top of it.
Rev. He who overcomes, him I will make a pillar in the
3:12 temple of My God, and he shall by no means go out
anymore, and I will write upon him the name of My
God and the name of the city of My God, the New
Jerusalem,...and My new name.

Jacob's dream is a most crucial point in Genesis, and 28:10-22
unveils the most crucial matter in the revelation of God. God desires to have a house on earth, and His intention is to transform
His called ones into stones, material for His building. In the ac-
count of Jacob's dream, the stone (vv. 11, 18, 22), the pillar (v. 18),
the house of God (vv. 17, 19, 22), and the oil (v. 18) are outstanding
items. The stone symbolizes Christ as the foundation stone, the
top stone, and the cornerstone for God's building (Isa. 28:16;
Zech. 4:7; Acts 4:10-12). It also symbolizes the transformed man,
who has been constituted with Christ as the transforming element to be the material for the building of God's house (Gen. 2:12;
Matt. 16:18; John 1:42; 1 Cor. 3:12; 1 Pet. 2:5; Rev. 21:11, 18-20),
which is the church today (1 Tim. 3:15) and which will consummate in the New Jerusalem as the eternal dwelling place of God
and His redeemed elect (Rev. 21:3, 22). (Gen. 28:12, footnote 1)

Today's Reading

If Jacob had not called this pillar the house of God, we would
never realize that the pillar of stone was for the building of God's
house....Now we know that this stone can become a house. This
indicates that the pillar will become a building, the house of God.

In the book of Genesis, there are two kinds of pillars—the pillar
of stone (28:18; 35:14) and the pillar of salt (19:26). Which kind of
pillar do you want to be? Certainly, we all want to be pillars of stone.
The pillar of stone indicates building in strength. Solomon set up
two pillars in the porch of the temple (1 Kings 7:21). The first pillar
was named Jachin, which means "He shall establish," and the

second was named Boaz, which means "in it is strength." The pillar of stone not only indicates building, but building in strength. The pillar of salt indicates shame, for a pillar of salt is useless for God's purpose. Lot's wife, who was one of God's called people, became a pillar of shame. She should have been building material, but due to her degradation she became shameful material.

Although in Genesis 28 Jacob was a supplanter, by the time we come to chapter 48 we see that this supplanter has been thoroughly transformed into a man of God. This man of God is the pillar. In a sense, the house of God was built with this pillar. When you enter into the temple of God in the universe, the first thing you see is this God-man, this Israel standing before God's building. After Jacob was transformed into Israel, he stood in front of God's building as a signboard of God's house. (*Life-study of Genesis*, pp. 1049, 1051-1052)

[In Revelation 3:12] we see that the overcomer will be made a pillar built into the temple of God. Because he is built into God's building, "he shall by no means go out anymore." This promise will be fulfilled in the millennial kingdom as a prize to the overcomer.

In Revelation 3:12 the word *make* is very significant. The Lord says that He will make the overcomer into a pillar. The Lord makes us pillars by transforming us, that is, by carrying away our natural element and by replacing it with His divine essence. Therefore, the meaning of *make* in 3:12 is to constitute us into something, to construct us in a creative way. In the church life today the Lord is making us, constituting us, into pillars in the temple of God. The Lord's work in the church is to work Himself into us as the divine flow to carry away our natural being and replace it with His substance that we may be gradually processed by His transforming element. As the result of this transforming work, we become pillars in the temple of God. (*The Conclusion of the New Testament*, p. 1215)

Further Reading: Life-study of Genesis, msg. 82

Enlightenment and inspiration: _____

_____

_____

_____

Morning Nourishment

Rom.   And do not be fashioned according to this age, but
12:2   be transformed by the renewing of the mind that
        you may prove what the will of God is, that which
        is good and well pleasing and perfect.
1 Tim. But if I delay, *I write* that you may know how one
3:15   ought to conduct himself in the house of God, which
        is the church of the living God, the pillar and base of
        the truth.

Revelation 3:12 tells us that the overcomers will be pillars in the temple of God in the coming age. However, Revelation 21:22, speaking of the New Jerusalem in the coming age and in eternity, says, "I saw no temple in it, for the Lord God the Almighty and the Lamb are its temple." Here we see that in the New Jerusalem the Triune God Himself will be the temple. This means that for the overcomers to be pillars in the temple means that they will be pillars in the Triune God. This involves being mingled with the Triune God and constituted of Him. This is a mystery.

Even in today's church life, the overcoming saints are pillars in the Triune God. (*The Conclusion of the New Testament*, pp. 1215-1216)

Today's Reading

The thought concerning the pillar in the book of Genesis is that of testimony. After Jacob had arranged a settlement with Laban, he "took a stone and set it up as a pillar" (31:45), and this pillar was a testimony (vv. 51-52). Undoubtedly, when Jacob set up the pillar in chapter 28, his concept was also that of a testimony. Under the inspiration of the Spirit of God, he said that this testimony would be the house of God. The temple in the Old Testament certainly was a testimony to God. The principle is the same with respect to the church today. According to 1 Timothy 3:15, the house of God, which is the church, is the pillar. This means that the church as a whole stands on earth to testify God to the universe.

By having Christ wrought into our being, we become material for the building. First, the stone for the pillar is Christ. Following this, it is Christ experienced by us and wrought into us. Now this stone is not merely Christ, but Christ within us. Christ is wrought into our being, and we become one with Him. In this way, we become the building material for the pillar.

The working of Christ into our being is true transformation. When the element of Christ is added into us, we become the material for the building of the pillar.

According to Genesis 28:18, Jacob "took the stone that he had put under his head, and he set it up as a pillar." The pillar was the stone he had used for a pillow. This stone depicts Christ as our rest.

We have seen that Jacob took a stone and made it his pillow. For years I could not understand the significance of this.... After being saved we might have had troubles. Nevertheless, deep within, we had the assurance that there was a solid rock upon which we could rest. This solid rock is the very nature, the very element of Christ, which has been wrought into our being.

As men, we were made from the dust of the ground (2:7). Romans 9 indicates that we are vessels of clay, not of stone. If I had been Jacob, I would have made a pile of clay and rested upon it. In God's eyes, however, clay can never be our rest. Our human life, our natural human life and being, cannot be our rest. It does not matter how well educated we are nor what position we have. As long as we do not have the divine nature within us, we are merely clay. This clay cannot be our solid support. None of us found rest until we were saved. On that day, something divine, something of Christ, was wrought into us and became the solid support within us. This is our rest, our pillow. Our pillow is the divine element, the very Christ, which has been wrought into our being. As we were taking our human journey, we suddenly had a dream in which Christ Himself was wrought into us. Christ's nature is the rock which has been wrought into our nature of clay. Hence, we have a rock upon which we can lay our head. (*Life-study of Genesis,* pp. 1064, 1059, 1058, 932-933)

Further Reading: Life-study of Genesis, msg. 83

Enlightenment and inspiration: _____

_____

_____

Morning Nourishment

Gal. I am crucified with Christ; and *it is* no longer I *who*
2:20 live, but *it is* Christ *who* lives in me; and the *life* which I
now live in the flesh I live in faith, the *faith* of the Son
of God, who loved me and gave Himself up for me.

1 Cor. But by the grace of God I am what I am; and His
15:10 grace unto me did not turn out to be in vain, but, on
the contrary, I labored more abundantly than all of
them, yet not I but the grace of God which is with me.

After having the dream, Jacob set up the stone for a pillar
(Gen. 28:18). The stone upon which we lay our head must become building material. Before coming into the church life, we
could not understand this. But now, having come into the church,
we realize that the very stone upon which we lay our head for
rest must become a pillar, that is, the stone must become the
material for God's building. Praise the Lord that we have been
saved and are at rest. But what about God's rest? He cannot
have rest until the stone upon which we rest our head has been
set up to be a pillar for His building. God will not set up this
pillar—we must do it. Our pillow must be set up to be a pillar. In
other words, our experience of Christ must become a pillar.

After coming into the church life, day by day we are setting
up our experience of Christ to be a pillar. It is no longer just a
pillow but a pillar. It is not only a matter of our rest; it is a
matter of God's building for His rest. (*Life-study of Genesis,*
pp. 933-934)

Today's Reading

The two pillars in front of the temple in the Old Testament
were a strong testimony of God's building.

Now we come to a crucial point—the two pillars were
made of bronze (1 Kings 7:15). In Genesis the pillar is a pillar
of stone, but in 1 Kings 7 the pillars are pillars of bronze. A
stone indicates transformation. Although we are clay, we can
be transformed into stone. But what does bronze signify? It
signifies God's judgment. For example, the altar at the en-

trance of the tabernacle was covered with bronze indicating God's judgment (Exo. 27:1-2; Num. 16:38-40). The laver was also made of bronze (Exo. 30:18). Furthermore, the serpent of bronze put on a pole (Num. 21:8-9) also testified of Christ's being judged by God on our behalf (John 3:14). Therefore, in typology, bronze always signifies God's judgment. That the two pillars were made of bronze clearly indicates that if we would be a pillar, we must realize that we are those under God's judgment. We should not only be under God's judgment, but also under our own judgment. Like Paul in Galatians 2:20, we must say, "I have been crucified. I have been crucified because I am not good for anything in God's economy. I am only qualified for death." Many brothers are intelligent and capable, and many sisters are quite nice. Nevertheless, we must recognize that actually we are not good at all. We are not even worth a penny. We are only good for death. To say, "I have been put aside, condemned, and put to death," is a type of self-judgment. What is your judgment regarding yourself? You must answer, "My judgment of myself is that I am good for nothing and that I have been crucified."

If you think that you are qualified to be a pillar, then you are already disqualified.

In Galatians 2:20 Paul said, "It is no longer I who live, but it is Christ who lives in me." We may also apply his word in 1 Corinthians 15:10, which says, "But by the grace of God I am what I am; and His grace unto me did not turn out to be in vain, but, on the contrary, I labored more abundantly than all of them, yet not I but the grace of God which is with me."...Paul seemed to be saying, "Whatever I am, I am by the grace of God. By myself, I am nothing. By myself, I could never be an apostle or a minister of God's living word. I labored more than the others, but it was not I who labored—it was the grace of God." This is the experience of bronze. (*Life-study of Genesis,* pp. 1064-1065, 1067)

Further Reading: Life-study of Genesis, msg. 84

Enlightenment and inspiration: _____

_____

_____

_____

Morning Nourishment

Matt. Then Jesus said to His disciples, If anyone wants
16:24 to come after Me, let him deny himself and take up
his cross and follow Me.

S. S. I am a rose of Sharon, a lily of the valleys. As a lily
2:1-2 among thorns, so is my love among the daughters.

Our problem is that we do not condemn ourselves. Rather, we
vindicate, justify, approve, and excuse ourselves. Often we say,
"That is not my mistake; it is Brother So-and-so's mistake. I am
always careful. I am not wrong." This is self-vindication. After we
vindicate ourselves, we proceed to justify and approve ourselves.
We do not need to be tested, for we have already approved ourselves. In our eyes, there is no problem with ourselves. Sometimes,
however, we are caught in a mistake. Then we excuse ourselves,
perhaps by saying, "I made that mistake because the meeting was
so long and I was tired." How often we make exits for ourselves! We
have four big exits: self-vindication, self-justification, self-approval,
and self-excuse. Even when we are caught in a mistake, we still
excuse ourselves. For example, a sister may say, "I type poorly
because the others have the best typewriters and the worst type-
writer is allotted to me." In the past, I have had a lot of self-vindication, self-justification, self-approval, and self-excuse....If we
would daily crucify these four things, there would be no fighting
whatever in our homes. (*Life-study of Genesis,* p. 1071)

Today's Reading

First Kings 7:17 speaks of "nets of checker work with
wreaths of chain work for the capitals that were at the top of
the pillars, seven for the one capital, and seven for the second
capital." To what do the nets of checker work and wreaths of
chain work refer? After consulting many versions, I discovered
that the checker work resembles a trellis, a frame with small
square holes that bears a vine. Furthermore, the word *work* in
this verse implies a design. Hence, checker work is a checker
design and chain work a chain design. As we shall see, this
checker design is for the growth of the lilies. This trellis is the

setting for the lilies. In a sense, it is a net to hold the lilies. The chain work is like a wreath encompassing the outside of the capital. Hence, upon the capitals are nets of checker work and wreaths of chain work.

What does all this signify? We have seen that the number five, the height of the capitals, denotes responsibility, and that two times five means fullness of responsibility. But why are there also on these capitals nets of checker work and wreaths of chain work? While I was burdened to understand this, the Lord showed me that this is the intermixed and complicated situation. The burden and responsibility borne by the pillars in the family, in the church, and in the ministry is always in a complicated and intermixed situation.

In order to bear the responsibility in this complicated situation, we must live by faith in God. First Kings 7:19 says, "And the capitals that were at the top of the pillars in the portico were of lily work." The lily signifies a life of faith in God. First, we must condemn ourselves, realizing that we are fallen, incapable, unqualified, and that we are nothing. Then we must live by faith in God, not by what we are or by what we can do. We must be a lily existing by what God is to us, not by what we are (Matt. 6:28, 30). Our living on earth today depends upon Him. How can we possibly bear the responsibility in the intermixed and complicated church life? In ourselves, we are incapable of doing this, but we can do so if we live by faith in God. It is not I, but Christ who lives in me—this is the lily. It is not I who bear the responsibility—it is He who bears it. I live, not by myself but by Him, and I minister, not by myself but by Him.

On the one hand, we are the condemned and judged bronze; on the other hand, we are the living lilies. The bronze means "not I," and the lily means "but Christ." Those who are lilies can say, "The life that I now live, I live by the faith of Jesus Christ." (*Life-study of Genesis,* pp. 1073-1075)

Further Reading: Life-study of Genesis, msg. 87

Enlightenment and inspiration: _____

_____

_____

_____

Morning Nourishment

Eph. And He Himself gave some as apostles and some as
4:11-12 prophets and some as evangelists and some as
shepherds and teachers, for the perfecting of the
saints unto the work of the ministry, unto the
building up of the Body of Christ.

First Kings 7:20 says, "So then the capitals that were on the
two pillars were above and close to the bulge that was beside the
network. And there were two hundred pomegranates, in rows
around both capitals." Hallelujah for the two hundred pomegranates! Around each capital was a projection, like a bulge. Encompassing the projection on each capital were two rows of a hundred
pomegranates each. This indicates two times of a hundredfold
expression of the riches of life. If you contact these elders who
daily bear the responsibility in the intermixed and complicated
situation, you will see that they express pomegranates, the riches
of life. All the complaints, dissatisfactions, and troubling tele-
phone calls eventually form a projection full of pomegranates.
How wonderful this is! (*Life-study of Genesis,* p. 1076)

Today's Reading

If you read all the portions concerning the two pillars, you will
realize that the bowls are composed of the network, the chain
work, the lilies, and the pomegranates. The pomegranates are not
on the base of the capital but on the chain work surrounding the
bowls. The network covers the bowls, the chain work surrounds
the bowls, the pomegranates are upon the chain work, and the lily
grows upon the network. All these things together are the bowl. If
you consider this in the light of your experience, you will realize
that through the crossing out by the network and the restriction
of the chain work, you live as a lily to express the riches of the life
of Christ. This is a living testimony coming out of the process of
resurrection. (*Life-study of Genesis,* p. 1082)

In spiritual significance the bowls of the capitals are a testimony (two) indicating that those who place themselves under
God's judgment (bronze), counting themselves as nothing, are

able to bear responsibility (five) in full (ten) and express the riches of the divine life (pomegranates) in the midst of a complicated and intermixed situation (the checker work and chain work) out of the process of resurrection (the base of the capitals, three cubits in height) because they do not live by themselves but by God (lilies). (1 Kings 7:16, footnote 1)

The pillars of the temple were built by Solomon through Hiram, "a bronze worker" who was "full of wisdom and understanding and skill to do all kinds of work in bronze" (1 Kings 7:14). Much of what is found in the Old Testament, such as the tabernacle and the temple, is a shadow, a type. We need to know the fulfillment of all these types. Solomon was a type of Christ, and Hiram was a type of the gifted person in the New Testament. Undoubtedly, the apostle Paul was a gifted person; he was the New Testament Hiram.…[In Ephesians 4:11 and 12] the gifted persons are given by the Head to the Body to perfect the saints. That the pillars were not built by Solomon directly but by Solomon through Hiram indicates that today Christ does not build up the pillars directly but through the gifted persons. Thus, we must submit to the hands of the gifted persons, just as the bronze was subject to the skilled and gifted hands of Hiram. (*Life-study of Genesis*, pp. 1063-1064)

Second Chronicles 2:14…says that Hiram's mother was "a woman of the daughters of Dan." The tribe of Dan is the tribe of idolatry that caused God's people to stumble and fall from God's way (Gen. 49:17 and footnote). The fact that Hiram's mother was of Dan indicates that Hiram's origin, like that of all men, was of sin (Psa. 51:5; cf. John 8:44a). That Hiram became one who was "of the tribe of Naphtali," the tribe of resurrection, that is, of transformation (Gen. 49:21 and footnote), signifies that in order to be a part of God's building and participate in its building work, we need to be transferred from the "tribe of Dan" into the "tribe of Naphtali" by being regenerated and transformed in Christ's resurrection (1 Pet. 1:3; 2 Cor. 3:18). (1 Kings 7:14, footnote 1)

Further Reading: Life-study of Genesis, msgs. 85-86

Enlightenment and inspiration: _____

_____

_____

_____

Morning Nourishment

Gen. Naphtali is a hind let loose; he gives beautiful
49:21 words.
Hab. Jehovah the Lord is my strength; and He makes
3:19 my feet like hinds' *feet* and will cause me to walk
on my high places...

In Genesis 49:21 Jacob spoke of Naphtali with high favor. A
hind does not seem to be related to beautiful words. But we
must not understand the Bible according to our natural mind;
we must understand the Bible according to the Bible.

A hind signifies a person who trusts in God in a desperate
situation....Those who trust in God and rejoice in God in the
midst of a desperate situation, a situation in which every
source of supply is cut off, are hinds.

Habakkuk 3:19 says, "Jehovah the Lord is my strength; /
And He makes my feet like hinds' feet / And will cause me to
walk on my high places." Those who trust in God walk, not in
the valleys, but upon the tops of the mountains. If you do not
know how to exercise faith in God when you are in a desperate
situation, at that time you will creep in the valleys. You will
never walk and skip upon the mountains. Only those who trust
in God when they are in a desperate situation can leap upon
the mountaintops. (*Life-study of Genesis,* pp. 1096-1097)

Today's Reading

The hind is also mentioned in the title of Psalm 22, which
says, "According to the hind of the dawn." This psalm is about
Christ in resurrection through crucifixion....In the Old Testament the hind refers not only to a person who trusts in God and
walks upon the mountaintops, but also to one who lives in resurrection for God's assembly, for the church life.

Naphtali also gives beautiful words. Naphtali was in the land
of Galilee (Matt. 4:15). All the first group of apostles came from
Galilee, and in Acts 1:11 they were addressed as "men of Galilee." Out from these Galileans, people of Naphtali, came beautiful words, that is, the preaching of the gospel. In the New

Testament we see that the word which came out of these Galileans was the word of life (Acts 5:20), the word of grace (14:3), the word of salvation (13:26), the word of wisdom (1 Cor. 12:8), the word of knowledge (v. 8), and the word of building (Acts 20:32). (*Life-study of Genesis,* pp. 1097-1098)

Tyre was a Gentile city noted for its commerce; hence, it was one with Satan (Ezek. 28:12, 16). Hiram's father was the source of Hiram's skill in working with bronze. However, his father died, leaving his mother, the source of his existence, a widow. This signifies that in order to be useful to God for the building of the church, God's dwelling place, we need to acquire the secular learning and skills but must allow our "Tyrian" father, the source of these things, to die. Furthermore, our "Danite" mother must be "widowed" (separated from the worldly source), and we must be of the "tribe of Naphtali," the tribe of transformation. Thus, we continue to possess the learning and the skills without the source, our existence (mother) is no longer linked to our worldly origin, and we are in resurrection. Moses and the apostle Paul are excellent examples of this principle. (1 Kings 7:14, footnote 2)

Hiram was brought from Tyre to King Solomon in Jerusalem (vv. 13-14), the place where the temple was to be built. Jerusalem typifies the church. Both today's Solomon (Christ) and God's present building are in the church. Thus, in order to be useful to God for His building, we must gain secular skills, live in resurrection, and come to the proper ground, the ground of the church. (1 Kings 7:14, footnote 3)

History records that Moses and Paul were more than useful in the hands of God. They were not only pillars; they were also pillar builders. This is the need in the church today. In order for this need to be met, we all must pray to the Lord, saying, "Lord, for the sake of Your building, make me a pillar and a pillar builder." (*Life-study of Genesis,* pp. 1117-1118)

Further Reading: Life-study of Genesis, msg. 88; *The Builder of the Pillars* (booklet)

Enlightenment and inspiration: _____

_____

_____

_____

Hymns, #1275

1   Glorious things to thee are spoken,
     Philadelphia, church of love.
  These things saith the One who's holy,
     He who's real speaks from above;
  He that has the key of David,
     Who the kingdom's entrance won,
  "I will open, no man shutteth"—
     He has spoken; it is done.

2   Hallelujah, Philadelphia,
     Thine are works that please the Lord.
  Strength thou hast, though just a little,
     And hast kept His living Word.
  Thou His holy name denied not,
     But confessed it here below—
  Lo, a door is set before thee,
     Through which none but thee can go.

3   Thou, beloved Philadelphia,
     Dost His Word of patience keep.
  From the hour of trial He'll save thee,
     Which o'er all the world shall sweep.
  Troublers too shall know He loves thee;
     They to thee must then bow down.
  "Hold thou fast, for I come quickly,
     That no man may take thy crown."

4   Hallelujah, overcomers,
     "In the temple of My God,
  I will build them in as pillars,
     Nevermore to go abroad."
  God's own name is written on them
     And the new name of the Lord.
  With the Triune God they're blended;
     They're the city of our God.

5   Hallelujah, out of heaven,
     Comes the New Jerusalem:
  Gates of pearl and walls of jasper,
     Mingled with each precious gem.
  Philadelphia, Philadelphia,
     Has become His bride so dear.
  Now the Spirit in the churches
     Speaks to all who have an ear.

Composition for prophecy with main point and sub-points: _____

_____

_____

_____

_____

_____

_____

_____

_____

_____

_____

_____

_____

_____

_____

_____

_____

_____

_____

_____

_____

_____

_____

_____

_____

_____

_____

_____

_____

_____

_____

_____

⌐

*Living Christ by Walking
according to the Spirit for the Body Life*

Scripture Reading: Gal. 2:20; Eph. 3:17a; Phil. 1:21a; Rom.
8:4; 12:4-5

Day 1
&
Day 2

I. **We need to live Christ in and for the church
life (Gal. 1:2, 15-16; 2:20; 4:19):**

A. The central thought of the Bible is that God
desires us to live Christ for the building up of
the Body of Christ (Phil. 1:21a; Eph. 4:12, 16):

1. The main point of our Christian life is to
live Christ.

2. The climax, the highest point, of the divine
revelation in the entire Bible is to live Christ.

B. In the New Testament there are four main verses
that reveal the matter of living Christ (John
6:57; 14:19; Gal. 2:20; Phil. 1:21a).

C. The Christian life is the life in which the believers of Christ live Him (v. 21a).

✶ D. Our primary concern should not be anything
outward but whether we are living the self or
living Christ (Gal. 2:20):

1. We are often distracted by outward things,
such as our work or the problems in the
local churches.

2. Actually, such problems are mainly due to a
lack of living Christ.

✶ 3. When we are living Christ, we are best able
to care for the church.

E. If we would live Christ, we must take Him as our
person and be one person with Him (Eph. 3:17a;
Gal. 2:20):

1. He and we must be one in a practical way
(1 Cor. 6:17).

2. To live Christ is to live a person; we should
live a life that is Christ Himself.

F. We should focus our whole attention on living

Christ and care only to live Christ, not allowing anything to distract us from the direct, personal experience of Christ (Gal. 2:20; Phil. 3:9-12).

G. Living Christ requires that we love Him to the uttermost (Mark 12:30):

Lord Jesus I love you!

  1. Part of the secret of living Christ is telling the Lord again and again that we love Him (1 Cor. 2:9).
  2. If we do not love the Lord, we cannot live Him.

H. To live Christ means that when Christ lives, we who believe into Him and who are in Him also live (John 14:19):

  1. We live in Christ's living, and He lives in our living.
  2. If we live in His living, His living will also be in our living (Gal. 2:20).

Day 3 II. **The practical way to live Christ is to walk according to the spirit (Phil. 1:21a; Rom. 8:4):**

A. We need to pay our full attention to walking according to the spirit in order to live Christ.

B. The word *walk* in Romans 8:4 denotes the general walk in our living, including how we think, speak, act, and move.

C. The spirit in verse 4 is the regenerated human spirit indwelt by and mingled with the Spirit; this corresponds to 1 Corinthians 6:17:

  1. Christ as the Spirit is in our spirit, and we are one spirit with Him (v. 17).
  2. Therefore, we have a mingled spirit—our human spirit mingled with the divine Spirit.

D. Ultimately, the Bible requires only one thing of us—that we walk according to the mingled spirit (Rom. 8:4):

  1. The key to everything is found in the wonderful Spirit who is in our regenerated spirit and who has become one spirit with our spirit (John 3:6).

    2. To walk in the spirit is to do everything in our daily life according to the spirit (Rom. 8:4).

    3. To live in the spirit is to let Christ fill and saturate us until He permeates our whole being and is thereby expressed through us (Eph. 3:17a).

    4. The mutual abiding in John 15:4-5 is the practice of walking according to the spirit.

    5. When we walk according to the spirit, we spontaneously bear the cross (Matt. 16:24).

    6. All the things that happen to us test whether we are walking according to the spirit or the flesh (Rom. 8:4-5).

    7. The best way to silence Satan is to walk according to the spirit (Rev. 12:11).

E. We need a clear view from the heavens to see that what the Lord wants is a group of people who walk according to the spirit.

F. The primary concern of the leading ones should be to help the saints to live Christ by walking according to the spirit in their daily life (Rom. 8:4).

Day 4   G. When we are not walking according to the spirit in our daily life, we are walking according to the flesh (vv. 5-6):

    1. According to Romans 8, anything that is not according to the spirit is according to the flesh.

    2. There are only two sources and two conditions of our daily living—the spirit and the flesh.

H. Other aspects of our Christian life, such as preaching the gospel, should be the result of walking according to the spirit (v. 4):

    1. If we practice to continually walk according to the spirit throughout the day, everything else will spontaneously issue forth.

    2. Our gospel preaching and shepherding should be the issue of our walking according to the spirit (Matt. 24:14; John 21:15-17).

I. Our primary concern should not be how to do things but to see that God wants a people who live Christ by walking according to the spirit (Rom. 8:4).

J. In order to exhibit Christ in the meetings, we must gain Christ in our daily life by walking according to the spirit (1 Cor. 14:26; Phil. 3:8, 12; Rom. 8:4).

Day 5   K. The leading ones primarily need to walk according to the spirit in their daily life and help other saints to enter into this kind of living (v. 4; Phil. 3:17; Heb. 13:7):

1. The leading ones need to enter into the actual practice of walking according to the spirit.

2. They need to help others to balance their corporate enjoyment of the Lord with a personal daily life of walking according to the spirit (Phil. 3:17).

L. Unceasing prayer is the way to walk according to the spirit (1 Thes. 5:17):

1. The way to walk according to the spirit is to pray unceasingly, just as we breathe unceasingly; our walking according to the spirit is our spiritual breathing.

2. We can walk according to the spirit by consistent, unceasing, moment-by-moment prayer (Luke 18:1).

Day 6 III. **The more we walk according to the spirit, the more the Triune God will live in us so that we may live Him for the Body life (Rom. 8:4; 12:4-5):**

A. When we walk according to the spirit daily and moment by moment, the Triune God as the Spirit will have the opportunity to make His home in us, settle down in us, and take possession of and occupy our entire being (Eph. 3:17a):

1. We need to live the Triune God by allowing Him to indwell us, make His home in us,

and take full possession of our being by our
walking according to the mingled spirit (Gal.
4:19; Rom. 8:4).

2. All we need to do is to live the Triune God;
   everything else will be a spontaneous issue
   of our living the Triune God (John 14:19-20;
   15:4-5).

B. Romans 8 reveals that the Triune God lives in us
so that we may live Him; this should be the focus
of our Christian life.

C. The Body of Christ in Romans 12 issues from
the experience of walking according to the spirit
in Romans 8:

1. All the members of the Body of Christ should
   be persons who walk according to the spirit
   (12:4-5; 8:4).

2. In principle, if we do not walk according to
   the spirit, we cannot practically have the
   Body of Christ; the Body life is annulled by
   a fleshly walk.

3. All the believers are members of the Body,
   but the practicality of the Body depends on
   the believers' walk.

4. If we truly walk according to the spirit, we
   will spontaneously be in the Body life (v. 4;
   12:4-5).

D. We need to see one thing—that the goal of the
Lord's recovery is to recover Christ, who is the
embodiment of the Triune God to be our life and
who is the Spirit to live within us and make us His
living members so that His Body will be built up
(Col. 2:9; 3:4; 1 Cor. 15:45b; Gal. 2:20; Eph. 4:16).

Morning Nourishment

Gal. I am crucified with Christ; and *it is* no longer I *who*
2:20 live, but *it is* Christ *who* lives in me; and the *life*
       which I now live in the flesh I live in faith, the *faith*
       of the Son of God, who loved me and gave Himself
       up for me.
Phil. For to me, to live is Christ and to die is gain.
1:21

Paul's life was to live Christ. If we would live Christ, we
must take Him as our person and be one person with Him. He
and we must be one in a practical way. In Galatians 2:20 Paul
declares, "It is Christ who lives in me." For Paul, this was not a
mere doctrine; it was a fact. It should also be real to us that
Christ lives in us. Furthermore, we should abide in Him and
allow Him to abide in us.

To live Christ is not merely to have a holy life or to live holi-
ness. To live Christ is to live a person. We should simply live
Christ. We should live a life that is Christ Himself. In our
Christian life, quite often we are still the ones living our natu-
ral life. We are not living Christ. To live Christ is to let Christ
Himself live from within us.

In order to live Christ, we must take Him as our person and
as our life. Every morning we should pray, "Lord, I thank You
for another day to practice living You. Lord, in myself I cannot
do this. I ask You to remind me to live You and grant me the
grace that I need for this."...We should not care for holiness,
spirituality, or victory as things in themselves, and we should
not care for our natural virtues or attributes. Instead, we
should focus our whole attention on living Christ and care only
to live Christ so that He might be magnified in us. (*The Conclusion of the New Testament*, pp. 3482-3483)

Today's Reading

The central thought of the Bible is that God desires us to
live Christ for the building up of the Body of Christ. The main
point of our Christian life is to live Christ. To live Christ should
be our primary goal; all the troubles in our Christian life come

because of our not living Christ. We need to practice to live Christ, realizing that He is the life-giving Spirit in our spirit, until we live Christ habitually.

The climax, the highest point, of the divine revelation in the entire Bible is to live Christ. In order to live Christ, we must practice being one spirit with Him, and in order to practice being one spirit with Him, we must exercise our spirit to pray unceasingly. If we pray unceasingly from our spirit, "Lord, live in me; Lord, live through me," we will build up a habit of not living our self but Christ; then we will live Christ habitually. The habit of ✴ living Christ is the habit of prayer. Apart from unceasingly praying, we cannot live Christ. It is only by such continual prayer, such breathing prayer, that we can live Christ spontaneously. In order to have such a prayer life, we must watch and pray, praying at every time in spirit, watching unto prayer in all petition, and persevering in prayer (Matt. 26:41; Eph. 6:18; Col. 4:2). Moreover the foundation for us to pray is our love for the Lord. Because we love the Lord and seek Him, we like to contact Him, pray to Him, and call upon Him. Part of the secret of living Christ is telling the Lord again and again that we love Him.

Living Christ requires that we love Him to the uttermost. As we are engaged in our daily activities, our living should not be those activities but Christ. Our mind should be concentrated on Christ, but the concentration of our mind on Christ depends upon our love for Christ. This is the reason that the New Testament charges us to love Christ (Mark 12:30; Rev. 2:4-5; John 14:23; 21:15-17; 1 Pet. 1:8). If we do not love Christ, we cannot live Him; loving Him is the best way to concentrate our entire being on Him….We need Christ to captivate us to an extent that even in our dreams we would live Christ. (*The Conclusion of the New Testament*, pp. 3485-3486)

Further Reading: The Conclusion of the New Testament, msg. 346; *CWWL, 1991-1992*, vol. 2, "The Christian Life," ch. 1; *Life-study of Philippians*, msg. 6

Enlightenment and inspiration: _____

_____

_____

_____

Morning Nourishment

John As the living Father has sent Me and I live because
6:57 of the Father, so he who eats Me, he also shall live
because of Me.
14:19 Yet a little while and the world beholds Me no
longer, but you behold Me; because I live, you also
shall live.

In the New Testament there are four main verses—two in the
Gospels and two in the Epistles—that reveal the matter of living
Christ....John 6:57...is the first verse in the New Testament that
directly touches the matter of living Christ. The second verse
is...John 14:19....The phrase *because I live* means that Christ
lives in resurrection. *Yet a little while* indicates His death and that
He will live again in His resurrection. The clause *because I live,
you also shall live* indicates that because He lives in resurrection,
we also shall live with Him and by Him. In the New Testament
John 6:57 and 14:19 are the most basic verses in unveiling to us
how we can live because of Christ and with Christ. The third
verse, perhaps the best in the Epistles concerning our living
because of Christ and with Christ, is Galatians 2:20. It says, "I am
crucified with Christ; and it is no longer I who live, but it is Christ
who lives in me; and the life which I now live in the flesh I live in
faith." The fourth verse is Philippians 1:21, which says, "To me, to
live is Christ." (*CWWL, 1989,* vol. 3, "The Experience and Growth
in Life," p. 17)

Today's Reading

The Christian life is the life in which the believers of Christ
live Christ and magnify Him [Phil. 1:20b-21a].

It is also the life in which the Christians live Christ and magnify Him corporately in their locality as a local church to be a local
expression of Christ as a part of the universal Body of Christ.
(*CWWL, 1991-1992,* vol. 2, "The Christian Life," pp. 349, 357)

We need to humble ourselves to see that there is a shortage in
our daily life of a practical living according to the vision that we
have seen in Paul's Epistles....We are often distracted by outward

things, such as our work or the problems in the local churches. Actually, such problems are mainly due to a lack of living Christ.

Our daily walk does not adequately correspond to our vision concerning the central lane of Paul's completing ministry.... What the Lord wants in His recovery is not our building of halls but our living of Christ. Our primary concern should not be anything outward but whether we are living the self or living Christ.

We should not be satisfied with merely knowing the truth; we must also seek to experience it. Our living should not remain the same after listening to many messages....We need to consider whether we are daily practicing to walk according to the spirit [Rom. 8:4]. To walk according to the spirit is to live Christ. The Lord wants a people who have such a walk and such a living.

✱ Through the years the churches have had some growth in life, yet our living of Christ is not adequate. Moreover, our growth is slow because our living is short. Our growth may be helped or frustrated by our living.

As leading ones, we know from our experience that when we are living Christ, we are best able to care for the church. (*CWWL, 1982,* vol. 1, "The Importance of Living Christ by Walking according to the Spirit," pp. 384-385)

Philippians 1:21 says, "To me, to live is Christ and to die is gain." To say that we must live Christ is easy, and to understand this simple phrase is also easy, but for us to actually live Christ involves a great deal. To live Christ means that when Christ lives, we who believe into Him and who are now in Him also live. Christ lives, and we also live (John 14:19). This means that we live in Christ's living and that He lives in our living. If we live in His living, His living will be in our living also. This is the mingled living of two lives. God and man live together. (*CWWL, 1989,* vol. 3, "The Experience and Growth in Life," pp. 29-30)

Further Reading: CWWL, 1989, vol. 3, "The Experience and Growth in Life," chs. 3, 5-6; *CWWL, 1982,* vol. 1, "The Importance of Living Christ by Walking according to the Spirit," ch. 1

Enlightenment and inspiration: _____

_____

_____

_____

Morning Nourishment

Rom. That the righteous requirement of the law might be
8:4-6 fulfilled in us, who do not walk according to the
flesh but according to the spirit. For those who are
according to the flesh mind the things of the flesh;
but those who are according to the spirit, the things
of the Spirit. For the mind set on the flesh is death,
but the mind set on the spirit is life and peace.

In the past few years we have seen the matter of living Christ
(Phil. 1:21; Gal. 2:20). Recently, based on Romans 8:4, we have
seen the matter of walking according to the spirit, which is the
practical way to live Christ. We are often distracted from walking according to the spirit....We need to pay our full attention to
walking according to the spirit in order to live Christ.

When we face serious problems, we often pray desperately to
seek the Lord's leading. Before we give a message, it is easy to
pray. However, walking according to the spirit is different from
praying in difficult situations or before spiritual activities. To
walk according to the spirit is to do everything in our daily life
according to the spirit. We need to walk according to the spirit
moment by moment not only in big things but also in small
things, such as writing a letter or talking with our family at the
dinner table. If we cannot do or say something according to the
spirit, we should not do or say it. We must admit that we are
short of such a living. To pray only during the meetings or when
we face a great problem is not to walk according to the spirit. Our
walking according to the spirit in our daily living should be like
our breathing. If we do not live Christ or walk according to the
spirit, our spiritual activities may be a performance. We should
not act one way in the meetings and another way in our daily life.
(CWWL, 1982, vol. 1, "The Importance of Living Christ by Walking according to the Spirit," pp. 387-388)

Today's Reading

Christ being the Spirit in our spirit to give us life is a wonderful and genuine teaching according to the Bible. However, we

cannot stop with knowing this teaching—we need to go on. We should not merely keep this teaching in our mind in order to muse upon it. We must also experience it. Paul says in Romans 8:4, "That the righteous requirement of the law might be fulfilled in us, who do not walk according to the flesh but according to the spirit." This verse does not speak of knowing but of walking. The word *walk* in this verse denotes the general walk in our living, including how we speak, think, act, and move. Verse 5 refers to "those who are according to the spirit." This indicates that we need not only to walk but also to have our entire being according to the spirit. Verse 6 reveals that we need to set our mind on the spirit.

Most Christians think that we should walk according to the teachings in the Bible. However, according to Paul's word in Romans 8:4, we should walk according to the spirit. Bible teachers and translators are unable to say definitely whether the spirit in verse 4 is the Spirit of God or the spirit of man. The spirit in this verse is the regenerated human spirit indwelt by and mingled with the Spirit. This corresponds to 1 Corinthians 6:17, which says, "He who is joined to the Lord is one spirit." We need to walk according to this mingled spirit.

Christ as the Spirit is in our spirit, and we are one spirit with Him (Rom. 8:10, 16; 1 Cor. 6:17). Therefore, we have a mingled spirit—our human spirit mingled with the divine Spirit. Everyone who is saved has a mingled spirit within. We need to walk according to this mingled spirit. Regrettably, few believers know how to walk according to the spirit. Most know only to follow outward biblical teachings, such as being humble (Matt. 18:4). However, being outwardly humble in a religious way does not please the Lord. Our humility must come from walking according to the spirit. (*CWWL, 1973-1974,* vol. 2, pp. 440, 457)

Further Reading: CWWL, 1982, vol. 1, "The Importance of Living Christ by Walking according to the Spirit," ch. 2; *CWWL, 1973-1974,* vol. 2, pp. 437-443

Enlightenment and inspiration: _____

_____

_____

_____

Morning Nourishment

Rom. Because the mind set on the flesh is enmity against
8:7-9 God; for it is not subject to the law of God, for neither
can it be. And those who are in the flesh cannot please
God. But you are not in the flesh, but in the spirit, if
indeed the Spirit of God dwells in you. Yet if anyone
does not have the Spirit of Christ, he is not of Him.

When we are not walking according to the spirit in our daily life,
we are walking according to the flesh. According to Romans 8:4-9,
anything that is not according to the spirit is according to the flesh.
There are only two sources and two conditions of our living—the
spirit and the flesh. Outward behavior, such as whether we are loving or hating others or praising or criticizing others, does not deter-
mine whether we are living according to the spirit or the flesh.
Even our love is according to the flesh if it is not according to the
spirit. We may rarely speak negatively, but even our positive speech
that is not according to the spirit is still according to the flesh.

Perhaps it is difficult to know the spirit, but it is easy to know
what is not the spirit....In order to be able to live according to the
spirit, it is sufficient for us to know when our speech and actions
are not according to the spirit. However, we do not practice such a
life. During the meetings we may conduct ourselves according to
the spirit, but after the meetings we often feel free to speak and do
things according to the flesh. It is not sufficient merely to live mor-
ally or ethically or even to decide what to do based on the Spirit's
leading, for we may be led by the Spirit to do something but then do
it according to the flesh. We need to do everything according to the
spirit, thinking, speaking, and acting moment by moment according to the spirit. (*CWWL, 1982*, vol. 1, "The Importance of Living
Christ by Walking according to the Spirit," p. 388)

Today's Reading

Other aspects of the Christian life, such as preaching the
gospel, should be the result of our living Christ. If all the saints
live Christ by walking according to the spirit, there will be a
great increase in the church. Much gospel preaching will

spontaneously issue from our walking according to the spirit. Several years ago I proposed that the saints in a certain locality go out at least once a week to contact others. Everyone listened and agreed, but eventually no one practiced it. I found that it does not work to charge the saints to go out regularly to preach the gospel. However, if the elders in a locality take the lead to walk according to the spirit, and they minister such a life to the other saints, the saints in that locality will also walk according to the spirit and regularly preach the gospel.

Our primary concern should not be how to do things such as preaching the gospel and shepherding the new believers. Instead, we need to see that God wants a people who live Christ by walking according to the spirit. If we practice to continually walk according to the spirit throughout the day, everything else will spontaneously issue forth from such a living....Our gospel preaching and shepherding should not be activities but should be the issue of a daily life of walking according to the spirit....All such aspects of the Christian life should be part of our living. For instance, a daily life of walking according to the spirit will issue in our functioning with a released spirit in the meetings. If we do not live Christ in our daily life, we will have no surplus of Christ to bring to the meetings. In order to exhibit Christ, we must gain Christ in our daily life by walking according to the spirit. If the saints are living Christ, they will spontaneously function in the meetings.

We need a clear view from the heavens to see that what the Lord wants is a group of people who walk according to the spirit. The Lord's desire is not for many co-workers, elders, or activities, or much organization. As leading ones, we primarily need to walk according to the spirit in our daily life and help other saints to enter into this kind of living. (*CWWL, 1982,* vol. 1, "The Importance of Living Christ by Walking according to the Spirit," pp. 388-390)

Further Reading: CWWL, 1979, vol. 1, "Life Messages, Volume 2," chs. 62-64; *CWWL, 1993,* vol. 1, "The Move of God in Man," ch. 3

Enlightenment and inspiration: _____

_____

_____

_____

Morning Nourishment

1 Cor. **Therefore I make known to you that no one speak-**
12:3 **ing in the Spirit of God says, Jesus *is* accursed; and**
no one can say, Jesus *is* Lord! except in the Holy
Spirit.
1 Thes. **Unceasingly pray.**
5:17

When we walk according to the spirit daily and moment by moment, the Triune God as the Spirit will have the opportunity to make His home in our entire being. This is our greatest need.

The corporate aspect of the Christian life is certainly helpful, but what we often lack is a daily life of walking according to the spirit. The saints in a local church may experience a high corporate life for a time, but if they do not enter into the practice of walking according to the spirit, their enjoyment will eventually diminish. Many of us have experienced a high corporate life in the past. Today we need to enter into the actual practice of walking according to the spirit, and as leading ones, we need to help others to balance their corporate enjoyment of the Lord with a personal daily life of walking according to the spirit. Whether or not there is a high atmosphere of corporate enjoyment in our locality, we need to personally walk according to the spirit. Corporate exercise of the spirit helps our walking according to the spirit but cannot replace it. Our walking according to the spirit is our spiritual breathing, which is what enables us to endure. To stop breathing is an indication of death. We need to pay our full attention to walking according to the spirit, because our breathing is what matters. (*CWWL, 1982,* vol. 1, "The Importance of Living Christ by Walking according to the Spirit," pp. 390-391)

Today's Reading

Many saints need to practice walking according to the spirit in order to become less dependent on corporate help. The Lord may place us in an environment in which we do not have much opportunity to meet with others. The apostle John did not receive corporate help when he was in exile on the island of Patmos, but he was still in spirit (Rev. 1:10). We need to practice to be in spirit when we are alone. (*CWWL, 1982,* vol. 1, "The Importance of Living Christ by Walking according to the Spirit," p. 391)

The way to walk according to the spirit is to pray. When we pray in sincerity, we are in the spirit. The kind of prayer that we need to practice in order to walk according to the spirit is not the prayer that we have by setting aside a particular time and place to devote to prayer. If we pray only in this way, it is easy to come out of the spirit when our time of prayer is over. We need to pray unceasingly (1 Thes. 5:17), just as we breathe unceasingly. Unceasing prayer keeps us in our spirit.

The way to love the Lord and satisfy His desire to have a free way and all the ground within us is to pray unceasingly. We do not need to always pray for specific things. Instead, we need to practice unceasing prayer by calling on the Lord's name no matter what else we are doing. We should not call on the name of the Lord lightly or loosely. We need to call with some consideration, speaking to the Lord about what we are doing and thinking. Whenever we call on the Lord's name, we are in the Spirit (1 Cor. 12:3).

We need to continually walk and have our being according to the mingled spirit so that the indwelling Christ as the life-giving Spirit may have the opportunity to impart the riches of His life into every part of our being. In this way we will be transformed by being replaced with Christ. We can walk according to the spirit by constant, unceasing, moment-by-moment prayer. Before we do or say anything, we need to pray. Then we will be according to the spirit, and this will open the way for the Lord to impart Himself into us, spreading from our spirit into every part of our being and thereby transforming us as His life replaces our old life. In this way we will be replaced, transformed, and reconstituted with Christ to become His bride. (*CWWL, 1973-1974,* vol. 2, pp. 457-458, 443)

Further Reading: CWWL, 1973-1974, vol. 2, pp. 455-460

Enlightenment and inspiration: _____

_____

_____

_____

Morning Nourishment

Rom. That the righteous requirement of the law might
8:4 be fulfilled in us, who do not walk according to the
flesh but according to the spirit.

12:4-5 For just as in one body we have many members,
and all the members do not have the same function, so we who are many are one Body in Christ,
and individually members one of another.

We need to live Christ for His magnification by the bountiful
supply of the Spirit of Jesus Christ [Phil. 1:19]....The Spirit has
a rich provision to supply us in full to live Christ for His magnification. The bountiful supply of the Spirit of Jesus Christ contains all that the processed and consummated Triune God—
embodied in the all-inclusive Christ who is realized as the all-
inclusive Spirit—is, has, has accomplished, obtained, attained,
and will do. This bountiful supply of the Spirit is the un-
searchable riches of Christ to meet in time the need of the seekers of Christ. When we truly seek after Christ, we will receive
this bountiful supply. It is by such a bountiful supply of the Spirit
of Jesus Christ that the seekers of Christ, as His overcomers in
the consummation of this age, live Him for His magnification in
the New Testament economy of God for the producing and building up of the organic Body of Christ as the counterpart of the
consummated Triune God, which will consummate in the New
Jerusalem as His eternal enlargement and expression for eternity. (*The Conclusion of the New Testament,* pp. 3486-3487)

Today's Reading

Because the Triune God lives in us, we can live Him. This
needs to be our daily experience. Thus, the focus and central
teaching of the Bible is that the Triune God desires to live in His
redeemed and regenerated people so that they may live Him.

We simply need to consider whether we are living ourselves or
living God. If the leading brothers see this focus of the Bible and
begin to live God, many other saints will be brought into this kind
of living, and there will be a wonderful and spontaneous issue.

We need to live the Triune God by allowing Him to indwell us, make His home in us, and take full possession of our being and by walking according to the mingled spirit. When we see, appreciate, and practice this, the law of the Spirit of life will operate within us, our mind will spontaneously be set on the things of Christ, and our natural being with its strengths, habits, and practices will spontaneously be put to death. This is Romans 8— the Triune God living in us and our living the Triune God.

The Body of Christ in Romans 12 issues from the experience of walking according to the spirit in Romans 8. According to Paul's view of God's economy, all the members of the Body of Christ should be persons who walk according to the spirit. In principle, if we do not walk according to the spirit, we cannot practically have the Body of Christ. All the believers are members of the Body of Christ, but the practicality of the Body depends on the believers' walk. If the believers walk according to the flesh, although they are still members of the Body of Christ, there will be no Body in their experience. The Body life is annulled by a fleshly walk. There are millions of believers today, but there is very little of the Body life among them, because few walk according to the spirit.

We must reject all the false replacements of the one thing that is real and that counts—the Triune God living in us so that we may live Him....Nothing matters or will last other than the Triune God living in us and our living Him. We must refuse hierarchy, self-assumed authority, and human organization and care only for God's desire and the focus of His revelation in the Bible.

We all have to see one thing—that the goal of the Lord's recovery is to recover Christ, who is the embodiment of the Triune God to be our life and who is the Spirit to live within us and make us His living members so that His Body will be built up on the earth. (*CWWL, 1982,* vol. 1, "The Importance of Living Christ by Walking according to the Spirit," pp. 394, 397-398, 417, 409-410)

Further Reading: CWWL, 1982, vol. 1, "The Importance of Living Christ by Walking according to the Spirit," chs. 3-5, 7

Enlightenment and inspiration: _____

_____

_____

_____

Hymns, #499

1   Oh, what a life! Oh, what a peace!
    The Christ who's all within me lives.
    With Him I have been crucified;
    This glorious fact to me He gives.
    Now it's no longer I that live,
    But Christ the Lord within me lives.

(Repeat the last two lines of each stanza.)

2   Oh, what a joy! Oh, what a rest!
    Christ now is being formed in me.
    His very nature and life divine
    In my whole being inwrought shall be.
    All that I am came to an end,
    And all of Christ is all to me.

3   Oh, what a thought! Oh, what a boast!
    Christ shall in me be magnified.
    In nothing shall I be ashamed,
    For He in all shall be applied.
    In woe or blessing, death or life,
    Through me shall Christ be testified.

4   Oh, what a prize! Oh, what a gain!
    Christ is the goal toward which I press.
    Nothing I treasure, nor aught desire,
    But Christ of all-inclusiveness.
    My hope, my glory, and my crown
    Is Christ, the One of peerlessness.

Composition for prophecy with main point and sub-points: _____

_____
_____
_____
_____
_____
_____
_____
_____
_____
_____
_____
_____
_____
_____
_____
_____
_____
_____
_____
_____
_____
_____
_____
_____
_____
_____
_____
_____
_____
_____
_____
_____
_____
_____
_____
_____
_____
_____

The Heart and Spirit of a Leading One

Scripture Reading: Ezek. 36:26-27; Matt. 5:3, 8; Eph. 3:16-17, 20-21; Rev. 1:10; 4:2; 17:3; 21:10

Day 1   I. **God's promise to His chosen ones was that He would give them a new heart and a new spirit and that He would put His Spirit within them (Ezek. 36:26-27):**
   A. We all need a new start to maintain the newness of our heart and our spirit (2 Cor. 4:16; Rom. 7:6; cf. Prov. 4:23; 1 Pet. 3:4).
   B. Our heart is our loving organ, and our spirit is our receiving organ; while we are in a fallen or backslidden state, our heart toward the Lord is stony and hard, and our spirit is deadened (Eph. 2:1; 4:18).
   C. When the Lord saves us or revives us, He renews our heart, making our stony heart a heart of flesh, a heart that is soft and loving toward Him; furthermore, He enlivens and renews our spirit with His divine life (cf. 2 Cor. 3:3; Col. 2:13).
   D. As a result, we love the Lord and desire Him with our renewed heart, and we can contact Him, receive Him, and contain Him by exercising our renewed spirit.

II. **The New Testament begins by speaking of our heart and our spirit (Matt. 3:2; John 3:6):**
   A. John the Baptist first preached the gospel in the New Testament by declaring, "Repent, for the kingdom of the heavens has drawn near" (Matt. 3:2):
      1. According to the Greek, to repent is to have a change in our mind or a turn in our thinking; because the mind is the main part of the heart, to repent is a matter of the heart.
      2. A thoroughly repentant heart will become a new heart; because our God is a God of life

and is all-powerful, He gives us a new heart by transforming our heart (2 Cor. 3:16, 18).

B. A softened heart is a transformed heart, a new heart; we believers need to repent again and again; every time we repent, our heart will be more transformed and renewed; in Revelation 2 and 3 the Lord repeatedly calls the churches to repent (2:5, 16, 21-22; 3:3, 19).

Day 2 III. **As a leading one, a person must have an enlarged heart:**

A. A leading one must be large in heart (Psa. 119:32):

1. We must be genuine ministers of the new covenant, having an enlarged heart with the intimate concern of the ministering life, which is a fruitful life (2 Cor. 7:2-3):

   a. With an enlarged heart the apostles were able to embrace all believers regardless of their condition, and with an opened mouth they were able to speak to all believers frankly concerning the real situation into which they had been misled (6:11).

   b. This kind of openness and enlargement is needed to reconcile, to bring back, the misled or distracted believers to God.

2. Solomon was competent to oversee God's people because he had wisdom and a large heart, which are two aspects of one thing:

   a. Though he only asked for the wisdom and knowledge to go out and come in among God's people (1 Kings 3:5-9; 2 Chron. 1:10), God gave him "largeness of heart, even as the sand that is on the seashore" (1 Kings 4:29).

   b. The seashore encloses the sea, God having "set the sand as a boundary for the sea" (Jer. 5:22); this shows that Solomon's heart was larger than the sea.

B. There are difficulties in many local churches today because the elders do not have a large heart; pride, an expression of foolishness, comes from having a narrow heart:

1. Pride is an attribute of our fallen nature by birth.

Day 3

2. Even with Paul, the Lord was wary of his exceeding exaltation of himself, so He let him have a thorn in his flesh from Satan (2 Cor. 12:7-9).

3. Hence, the apostle Paul taught that a new convert should not be an overseer of the church, lest being blinded with pride he fall into the judgment prepared for the devil (1 Tim. 3:6).

4. Always remember that humility saves you from all kinds of destruction and invites God's grace (James 4:6).

5. Pride makes you a top fool.

6. Rivalry in the Lord's work is not only a sign of ambition but also a sign of pride.

7. Caring for your prestige and neglecting others' dignity are a sign of subtle pride.

8. Referring to your capacity, success, perfection, and virtue is a careless form of pride.

9. Thinking more highly of yourself than you ought to think is another form of pride and annuls the proper and organic order in the Body life (Rom. 12:3).

10. Christ in His humanity humbling Himself to wash His disciples' feet gives us a good model of how to humble ourselves to escape from pride (John 13:3-5).

11. Arguing about who is greater is an ugly form of pride (Mark 9:34).

12. Wanting to be great and not to be a servant and wanting to be the first and not to be a slave are also signs of pride (Matt. 20:26-27).

13. Lording it over the members of your church

under your shepherding is a strong sign of
your pride (1 Pet. 5:3).

14. The apostle Paul presented us with a good
model (1 Tim. 1:16):
a. He preached Christ as the Lord and himself as the believers' slave for the Lord's
sake (2 Cor. 4:5).
b. He testified that whoever was weak, he
also was weak, and that to the weak he
became weak that he might gain the weak
(11:29; 1 Cor. 9:22).

15. To restore a brother, overtaken in some of-
fense, with meekness (a gentle expression
of humility) protects us from being tempted
also (Gal. 6:1).

16. Self-boasting, self-exaltation, self-glorifica-
tion, and lusting after vainglory are all ugly
and base expressions of pride (5:26).

C. In order to enlarge their heart, the leading ones
in different localities should go to visit other
places; if circumstances allow, it would be even
better to travel overseas; the more we participate in the Lord's move, the more we see (Ezek.
1:15-21).

D. The ability to forgive others when they have
offended you is a matter of largeness of heart; if
we have an argument with a brother, it is mostly
because of the narrowness of our heart (Matt.
6:14-15).

Day 4   **IV. The Lord Jesus followed John the Baptist by
teaching that we need to be born of the Spirit
in our spirit (John 3:6):**

A. Our spirit is born again when God as the Spirit
enters into it to regenerate us with the divine
life; to be regenerated is to have the divine, eternal life (in addition to the human, natural life) as
the new source and new element of a new person.

B. We need to repent in order to have a new heart,
and we need to believe into the Lord Jesus so

that our spirit will be reborn to become a new spirit.

C. We need a loving heart and a powerful spirit (Mark 12:30; 2 Tim. 1:7).

D. A leading one must be a spiritual man with an exercised spirit; he must be dominated, governed, directed, led, and controlled by his spirit; a strong spirit is the main requirement for the leadership among God's people (1 Tim. 4:7; 1 Cor. 2:15; 14:32; John 4:24; 2 Cor. 2:13; Rom. 1:9; 8:16; 1 Cor. 6:17).

E. We can maintain the newness of our spirit by serving in newness of spirit (Rom. 7:6; 1:9) and by exercising our spirit of faith (2 Cor. 4:13); faith is in our spirit, which is mingled with the Holy Spirit (Rom. 8:16; 1 Cor. 6:17), not in our mind; doubts are in our mind.

Day 5   V. **We need to be pure in heart (Matt. 5:8) and poor in spirit (v. 3):**

A. We need a pure heart in order to see God, and we need a spirit that is emptied in order to receive the kingdom of the heavens.

B. To be pure in heart is to be single in our goal and aim; our goal should be God alone; even in our service and function in the church life, we should not have an intention to gain anything but God Himself.

C. If we come to a meeting with a sense that we are inwardly rich and have no need, this will close the door to God (Rev. 3:16-17, 20); we need to pray, "O Lord, thank You for always being with me, yet I am still short of You; I want to be emptied in my spirit so that You can have more room in me; O Lord, I open to You and ask You to gain more ground within my spirit."

VI. **We need to be strengthened into our regenerated spirit so that Christ may make His home in our hearts (Eph. 3:16-17):**

A. When a saved one is strengthened into his spirit

and possessed by Christ in his heart, deep within
he has a longing for the church life and an inner
consciousness concerning what the proper church
life is.

B. To know the church is not outward but absolutely inward; that the highways to Zion are in
our heart means that we need to take the way of
the church internally, not merely externally (Psa.
84:5).

Day 6　C. When we are strengthened through the Spirit
into our spirit and when Christ makes His home
in our heart, God is able to do superabundantly
above all that we ask or think concerning the
church life; if all the saints pray daily for this,
the glorious church life will spread and be prevailing throughout the United States and the
whole world (Eph. 3:20-21).

VII. **We need to be in our spirit in order to see the
visions in the book of Revelation:**

A. This book is composed of four major visions: the
churches (chs. 1—3), the destiny of the world
(chs. 4—16), Babylon the Great (chs. 17—20),
and the New Jerusalem (chs. 21—22); John was
in his spirit when he saw these four visions
(1:10; 4:2; 17:3; 21:10); we too need to be in our
spirit to see the visions in this book.

B. If we pray for thirty days that the Lord would
strengthen us into our spirit and take over our
heart, we will have a clear view and will be assured concerning the whole situation of the universe, including the church, the world, Babylon
the Great, and the New Jerusalem.

VIII. **The Lord's recovery depends upon our renewed, purified heart and our renewed,
strengthened spirit; when our heart is fully
possessed by Christ and our spirit is thoroughly saturated with the Spirit, God will
have a way, and the recovery will be prevailing.**

Morning Nourishment

Ezek. I will also give you a new heart, and a new spirit I
36:26-27 will put within you; and I will take away the heart
of stone out of your flesh, and I will give you a
heart of flesh. And I will put My Spirit within you
and cause you to walk in My statutes, and My ordinances you shall keep and do.

[Ezekiel 36:26-27] was God's promise to the children of Israel,
His called ones. They were distracted, but God called them back
with a promise that He would give them a new heart and a new
spirit. As God-created men they already had a heart and spirit,
but because they were distracted, their heart and spirit became
old. However, God would not give them up and came in to promise
them a new start by giving them a new heart and a new spirit. We
also need this new start today. (*CWWL, 1975-1976,* vol. 2, p. 337)

Our heart is our loving organ, and our spirit is our receiving
organ. While we are in a fallen or backslidden state, our heart
toward the Lord is stony and hard, and our spirit is deadened
(Eph. 2:1; 4:18). When the Lord saves us or revives us, He renews
our heart, making our stony heart a heart of flesh, a heart that is
soft and loving toward Him (cf. 2 Cor. 3:3). Furthermore, He enlivens and renews our spirit with His divine life (Col. 2:13). As a
result, we love the Lord and desire Him with our renewed heart,
and we can contact Him, receive Him, and contain Him by exercising our renewed spirit. (Ezek. 36:26, footnote 1)

Today's Reading

The New Testament begins by speaking of our heart and our
spirit. John the Baptist first preached the gospel in the New Testament by declaring, "Repent, for the kingdom of the heavens
has drawn near" (Matt. 3:2). According to the Greek, to repent is
to have a change in our mind or a turn in our thinking. The mind
is the main part of the heart. Therefore, to repent is a matter of
the heart. Our experience confirms this. The preaching of the
gospel in the New Testament began with the heart.

A thoroughly repentant heart will become a new heart.

Although God promised to give us a new heart, He does not take out our old heart and put in a new one like a surgeon performing a transplant. Because He is a God of life and is all-powerful, He gives us a new heart by transforming our heart. When we repent, something marvelous happens in our heart. We may feel that it is our doing when we say, "O God, I am utterly sinful. I am sorry. I repent before You. Please forgive me." On one hand, this is our doing, but on the other hand, while we are repenting, the wonderful God gets into us and transforms our heart. We may not have any consciousness that God is doing this marvelous work, but soon after we repent to Him, we discover that our heart is changed. It was previously hardened, but after we repent, we find that it has been softened.

When I was a teenager,...no one could change me or subdue me, but one day I repented. While I was walking on the street after hearing a gospel message, I spoke to the heavens, saying, "God, I made a great mistake to not want You before. Now I want You. I love You. I repent for the past." When I arrived home, I discovered that my heart had changed, for it was softened. My mother also noticed this change and marveled to see it. To be softened in our heart is a sign that we have truly repented. A softened heart is a transformed heart, a new heart.

Repentance is not something that only unbelievers need. We believers need to repent again and again. We may need to repent for not loving the Lord enough. Every time we repent, our heart will be more transformed and renewed. Repenting is like washing our hands—once is not enough. We need to repent all the time. In Revelation 2 and 3 the Lord repeatedly calls the churches to repent (2:5, 16, 21-22; 3:3, 19). We need to repent, because repentance is the best dose to heal our heart and the best way to regulate our heart. Repenting renews our heart. (*CWWL, 1975-1976,* vol. 2, pp. 337-338)

Further Reading: CWWL, 1975-1976, vol. 2, pp. 337-345; *CWWL, 1970,* vol. 1, pp. 431-437

Enlightenment and inspiration: _____

_____

_____

Morning Nourishment

2 Cor. Our mouth is opened to you, Corinthians; our heart
6:11-13 is enlarged. You are not constricted in us, but you are
constricted in your inward parts. But for a recompense in kind, I speak as to children, you also be enlarged.
Psa. I run the way of Your commandments, for You
119:32 enlarge my heart.

With an enlarged heart [the all-mature and all-fitting apos-
tles] were able to embrace all believers regardless of their condition, and with an opened mouth they were free to speak to all
believers frankly concerning the real situation into which they
had been misled. This kind of openness and enlargement is
needed to reconcile, to bring back, the misled or distracted believers to God. (2 Cor. 6:11, footnote 1)

Today's Reading

Largeness is the first necessary condition of an elder's heart.
In the Bible, there is one very good ruler, King Solomon. All read-
ers of the Bible admit that he is a standard and a typical character concerning administration in the Bible. If we want to find a
standard character on experiencing the cross, we have to go to
David. But to find a standard character on managing God's people, we have to go to Solomon....King Solomon was competent at
managing for two reasons: he had wisdom, and he had a large
heart. Actually, these are two aspects of one thing.

You will recall that Solomon succeeded to the throne when he
was very young. As soon as he succeeded to the throne, he went
to offer sacrifices to God. In the night, while God appeared to
him, Solomon prayed, "And now, O Jehovah my God, You have
made Your servant king in the place of David my father, though I
am a little child; I do not know how to go out or come in....Give
therefore to Your servant an understanding heart to judge Your
people and to discern between good and evil" (1 Kings 3:7-9). He
wanted wisdom from God. Everyone knows that the most necessary thing in management is wisdom. To have cleverness is not

enough, because cleverness is common, whereas wisdom is extraordinary. Solomon deeply felt that for a young man to rule the myriads of God's people, he needed wisdom from God. That was why he sought for wisdom before God. Surprisingly, however, though he asked only for wisdom, God gave him, in addition to wisdom, also a large heart. First Kings 4:29 says, "And God gave Solomon wisdom and very much understanding and largeness of heart, even as the sand that is on the seashore." It says that largeness of heart is like the sand on the seashore. A Chinese proverb speaks of the heart being as large as the capacity of the sea, but here the heart is as large as the sand on the seashore. The seashore encloses the sea. The Scriptures say that God has "set the sand as a boundary for the sea" (Jer. 5:22). Therefore, Solomon's heart was larger than the sea.

At the time when God gave Solomon wisdom, He also gave him a large heart. We have to know that all wise ones have large hearts, and everyone with a narrow heart is a foolish person. If you want to be a foolish person, let me teach you a way: simply make your heart small. In the same principle, if you enlarge your heart, you will become the wisest person. You cannot separate a large heart from wisdom and prudence. This is why I say that these are two aspects of one thing.

Pride is an expression of foolishness. But from where does pride come? It comes from being narrow. When a person is narrow and his heart is narrow, it is easy for him to be proud. It is very hard for a person with a large heart to be proud....Pride is the expression of the narrowness of a person. Suppose you give a message unusually well one day, and as a result, you become proud. This pride proves your narrowness. If your heart is large, even if you have preached very well a thousand times, let alone only once, you would not feel anything. All foolishness proves that a person's heart is narrow, and all pride proves that you are too small. (*The Elders' Management of the Church,* pp. 39-40)

Further Reading: The Elders' Management of the Church, ch. 3

Enlightenment and inspiration: _____

_____

_____

Morning Nourishment

Matt. **For if you forgive men their offenses, your heav-**
6:14-15 **enly Father will forgive you also; but if you do not**
forgive men their offenses, neither will your Father
forgive your offenses.

A person who oversees God's people needs much wisdom, but the secret of wisdom is to have a large heart....You have no idea how much this matter affects those serving as elders. Many of your inaccurate judgments are caused by your narrow heart. On the surface it appears that you lack wisdom, but actually, the problem comes because your heart is narrow. When many matters are poorly managed, you may attribute the cause to your foolishness, but actually your foolishness comes from your narrow heart. If you would only enlarge your heart, immediately you would become a person of wisdom.

Therefore, brothers, learn to enlarge your heart in all things.... Whether in learning the truth, in seeking to be spiritual, in contacting the brothers and sisters, in discerning others, or in managing affairs, we must learn to be large. Whenever we touch the affairs of the church and whenever we touch any spiritual matter, we have to learn to be large in our heart. We need to continue to be large. Largeness can solve many problems. (*The Elders' Management of the Church,* pp. 40-41)

Today's Reading

Suppose today everyone else in the church knows about a certain matter, but this matter is concealed from you. In your heart would you blame others? If your heart is large, you will not do this. Otherwise, you will surely complain about it. Perhaps a brother offends you today. Are you able to let the matter go? It depends on whether your heart is large or small. Surely, if your heart is small, you will not be able to let it go. If it is large, you will be able to let it go. Everything in the church can be governed by this principle.

Brothers, there are difficulties in many local churches today because the elders do not have a large heart. Therefore, I fully agree that the elders in the different localities should go to visit other places....If circumstances allow, it would be even better to travel overseas. Once a man goes out for a visit, his heart will be enlarged. It is wrong to be proud, and it is wrong to be boastful. It is also wrong to strive to be large, but you must learn to enlarge your heart. It does not mean that to have a large heart is to be loose. You must still be strict with yourself, yet your heart toward others must be large.

Of course, the natural life can never learn this lesson....In order to enlarge our own heart, we need the Lord's abundant grace. Please remember that the ability to forgive others is a matter that has to do with the largeness of heart. The ability to bless the ones who curse us also has to do with a large heart. Your heart must be so large that whenever others offend you, you can forgive them as soon as they confess to you. Though others may persecute you and inflict harm on you, you can still love them. To be able to forgive others when they have offended you is something that has to do with a large heart.

Oh, the wisdom that comes from a large heart is immeasurable! In everything we do, it is right for us to be disciplined, and it is wrong to be presumptuous. But the most important thing is that our heart has to be large. If the heart is not large enough, you must prepare yourselves to make mistakes in the future; you will surely eat the fruit of regret. Suppose a brother asks you to do something today. If your heart is not large enough and you deny his request, you will surely regret it later. Or, if a brother asks for your forgiveness today, and you would not forgive him due to your narrowness in heart, you will surely regret it later. Therefore, brothers, your heart must be enlarged. We are narrow persons, but we must learn to enlarge our hearts. If you have an argument with a brother, eight or nine times out of ten it is because of the narrowness of your heart. In these years, I have not met many people with a large heart. (*The Elders' Management of the Church*, pp. 41-43)

Further Reading: Life-study of 2 Corinthians, msg. 44; How to Be a Coworker and an Elder and How to Fulfill Their Obligations, ch. 4

Enlightenment and inspiration: _____

_____

_____

_____

Morning Nourishment

John Jesus answered, Truly, truly, I say to you, Unless one
3:5-6 is born of water and the Spirit, he cannot enter into
the kingdom of God. That which is born of the flesh
is flesh, and that which is born of the Spirit is spirit.
2 Cor. And having the same spirit of faith according to
4:13 that which is written, "I believed, therefore I spoke,"
we also believe, therefore we also speak.

After John the Baptist began to preach the gospel by calling
men to repent in their heart, the Lord Jesus followed by teaching
that we need to be born of the Spirit in our spirit (John 3:6). To
repent in our heart is only the first step. Following repentance in
our heart, we need to be reborn in our spirit. A proper, balanced
man has a good heart and a proper spirit. A good heart is a
repenting, renewed, softened heart, and a proper spirit is a spirit
that is born again....When we repent, God comes in to touch our
heart; when we believe in the Lord, God enters into our spirit to
beget us with His life. (*CWWL, 1975-1976,* vol. 2, p. 338)

To be regenerated is to have the divine, eternal life (in addition to the human, natural life) as the new source and new element of a new person. (John 3:6, footnote 2)

Today's Reading

A proper heart and a proper spirit are a new heart and a new
spirit. We need to repent in order to have a new heart, and we
need to believe into the Lord Jesus so that our spirit will be
reborn to become a new spirit. God does not take away our old
heart and replace it with a new one but transforms our old heart
into a new one. In the same principle, He does not take away our
old spirit and replace it with a new one. Instead, when we believe
into the Lord, God as the Spirit comes into our spirit to beget our
spirit by bringing His life element into our spirit. In this way, our
old spirit becomes a new spirit. As believers, we have a new heart
and a new spirit; this makes us proper persons.

Mark 12:30 says, "You shall love the Lord your God from
your whole heart." Our heart needs to be a loving heart—loving

not the world but God. Second Timothy 1:7 says, "God has not given us a spirit of cowardice, but of power and of love and of sobermindedness." Our spirit should be powerful, loving, and sober. (*CWWL, 1975-1976,* vol. 2, pp. 339-340)

We need a strong spirit for the leadership in the churches. Many think that a leader needs knowledge, ability, and other attributes. These things do not mean much among God's people. In the leadership for God's move, what we are must be reduced, but the ultimate requirement is to have a strong spirit.

When a person who is fully built up in his spirit speaks for God, in a sense, there is no need for him to receive the power or inspiration of the Holy Spirit, for whatever he expresses from his spirit is something of God....The standard of the leadership among God's people is such a built-up human spirit.

Paul concluded his second Epistle to Timothy by saying, "The Lord be with your spirit" (4:22)....Only the Lord's presence is adequate for the leadership, and His presence is with us in our spirit. To be clever, kind, and careful does not make us adequate to be an elder. Only exercising our spirit can make us adequate as an elder.

For the leadership in the churches, we need to pay our full attention to building up our spirit. There is no excuse not to exercise our spirit. We may not have the inspiration of the Holy Spirit, but 1 Corinthians 14:32 says, "The spirits of prophets are subject to prophets." Therefore, we do not need to wait for inspiration....To say that we should not speak because others are more qualified or more experienced is to make an excuse because we have a weak spirit. If our spirit is strong, we will exercise our spirit to function in every meeting. (*CWWL, 1975-1976,* vol. 1, pp. 405-407)

Faith is in our spirit, which is mingled with the Holy Spirit, not in our mind. Doubts are in our mind....By the mingled spirit...the apostles lived a crucified life in resurrection for the carrying out of their ministry. (2 Cor. 4:13, footnote 2)

Further Reading: CWWL, 1975-1976, vol. 1, pp. 405-412

Enlightenment and inspiration: _____

_____

_____

_____

Morning Nourishment

Matt. Blessed are the pure in heart, for they shall see
5:8 God.
3 Blessed are the poor in spirit, for theirs is the kingdom of the heavens.
Eph. That He would grant you...to be strengthened with
3:16-17 power through His Spirit into the inner man, that
Christ may make His home in your hearts through
faith...

When the Lord was teaching His disciples on the mount, He
said, "Blessed are the pure in heart, for they shall see God" (Matt.
5:8), and, "Blessed are the poor in spirit, for theirs is the kingdom
of the heavens" (v. 3). To be poor in spirit does not mean to have a
poor spirit but to not be filled with things other than God. We
need a pure heart in order to see God, and we need a spirit that is
emptied in order to receive the kingdom of the heavens. We need
to be emptied in our spirit so that our spirit will have more capacity for God to come in. (*CWWL, 1975-1976*, vol. 2, p. 339)

Today's Reading

As believers, we have been renewed in our heart and regenerated in our spirit, but we still need to purify our heart and be
poor in spirit. To be pure in heart is to be single in our goal and
aim. Our goal should be God alone. If we are aiming at anything other than God, our heart is not pure but complicated. We
need to be simplified in our heart by seeking after nothing but
God. Even in our service and function in the church life, we
should not have an intention to gain anything other than God
Himself. If we are simplified to care only for God, our heart will
be pure in whatever we do. For our Christian walk, we need to be
pure in our heart, not having any goal besides God.

We also need to be poor in spirit. If we come to a meeting
with a sense that we are inwardly rich and have no need, this
will close the door to God. To be poor in spirit, we need to pray,
"O Lord, thank You for always being with me, yet I am still
short of You. I want to be emptied in my spirit so that You can

have more room in me. O Lord, I open to You and ask You to gain more ground within my spirit." Recently, after I gave a message, a young man came to challenge me with many questions. I sensed that the answers to his questions meant nothing to him because he was not humble but full in his spirit. After repenting in our heart and being regenerated in our spirit, we still need to be pure in heart and poor in spirit.

[In] Ephesians 3:16-17...our inner man is our regenerated spirit, where God has installed Himself. We need to be strengthened into this spirit, and our heart needs to be occupied by Christ....We need to check with ourselves concerning whether we are being strengthened into our spirit and whether we are allowing the Lord to take over our heart. We need to be strengthened with power through the Spirit into our spirit, and our heart needs to be possessed by the Lord so that He can make His home in it.

If we are being strengthened by the Spirit into our inner man and are being possessed by Christ as He makes His home in our heart, we will spontaneously enter into the proper church life.... As soon as believers are helped to be right in their heart and spirit, they begin to seek after the church, and it becomes easy for them to discern what the proper church life is. When a saved one is strengthened into his spirit and possessed by Christ in his heart, deep within he has a longing for the church life and an inner consciousness concerning what the proper church life is. To know the church is not outward but absolutely inward. (*CWWL, 1975-1976,* vol. 2, pp. 339-341)

[In Psalm 84:5] the highways to Zion signify our intention to enter into the church as the house of God....On the one hand, we have entered into God; on the other hand, we are still on the highways to enter into God. That the highways are in our heart means that we need to take the way of the church internally, not merely externally. (Psa. 84:5, footnote 1)

Further Reading: Lessons on the Eldership, vol. 1, lsn. 14

Enlightenment and inspiration: _____

_____

_____

_____

Morning Nourishment

Eph. But to Him who is able to do superabundantly
3:20-21 above all that we ask or think, according to the
power which operates in us, to Him be the glory in
the church and in Christ Jesus unto all the generations forever and ever. Amen.

[Ephesians 3:16-17] speaks of being strengthened into the inner man and Christ making His home in our heart....According to
the context [in verses 20 and 21], being strengthened into our spirit
and Christ making His home in our heart are for the church. When
we are strengthened through the Spirit into our spirit and when
Christ makes His home in our heart, God is able to do superabundantly above all that we ask or think concerning the church life.

Ephesians is a book concerning the church. Therefore, being
strengthened into the inner man and Christ making His home
in our heart are for the church. We praise the Lord that His recovery has come to the United States and that we have been
brought into this recovery. However, we need to allow God to
have a way among us by being strengthened into our spirit and
allowing Christ to take full possession of our heart. If all the
saints pray daily for this, within a few years the glorious church
life will spread and be prevailing throughout the United States.
(*CWWL, 1975-1976,* vol. 2, p. 342)

Today's Reading

The Lord's recovery is not an ordinary Christian work; it altogether depends on our heart and spirit. Electricity is powerful,
but in order for it to operate, wires are needed to transmit it. Similarly, God is powerful; He is able to do superabundantly above all
that we ask or think, but He needs our renewed heart possessed
by Christ and our renewed, regenerated, and strengthened spirit
in order to have a way.

The last book of the Bible, Revelation, is composed of four
major visions: the churches (chs. 1—3), the destiny of the world
(chs. 4—16), Babylon the Great (chs. 17—20), and the New
Jerusalem (chs. 21—22). The apostle John was in spirit when

he saw each of these visions. In 1:10-12 John says, "I was in spirit on the Lord's Day and heard behind me a loud voice like a trumpet, saying, What you see write in a scroll and send it to the seven churches....And I turned to see the voice that spoke with me; and when I turned, I saw seven golden lampstands." Being in spirit is the way to see the churches.

When John saw the second major vision, concerning the destiny of the world, he was also in spirit and saw God's throne in heaven (4:2). Whatever is happening on earth is under the sovereignty of the divine throne in the heavens. Seeing this was a great encouragement and comfort to the suffering apostle.

Next John was carried away in spirit into a wilderness to see the third major vision—Babylon, which is the apostate church (17:3). He saw it clearly. Ultimately, he was carried away in spirit onto a great and high mountain to see the New Jerusalem, the fourth and final major vision (21:10).

Our inner eyes will be opened if for a period of thirty days we daily pray, "Lord, strengthen me into my spirit and make Your home in my heart." We will see clearly the four major things going on in the universe: the churches, the world, Babylon the Great, and the New Jerusalem. The world will be judged by God, and Babylon the Great will fall, but the churches will become the New Jerusalem, which will remain forever....If we pray for thirty days that the Lord would strengthen us into our spirit and take over our heart, we will see God's economy. We will have a clear view and will be assured concerning the whole situation of the universe, including the church, the world, Babylon the Great, and the New Jerusalem.

The Lord's recovery depends upon our renewed, purified heart and our renewed, strengthened spirit. When our heart is fully possessed by Christ and our spirit is thoroughly saturated with the Spirit, God will have a way, and the recovery will be prevailing. (*CWWL, 1975-1976,* vol. 2, pp. 342-345)

Further Reading: CWWN, vol. 58, ch. 2

Enlightenment and inspiration: _____

_____

_____

_____

Hymns, #1134

1   Oh, strengthen my spirit, Lord Jesus,
     Oh, strengthen my spirit, I pray;
     Oh, strengthen my spirit with power
     And spread to my heart today.

     Into my heart, into my heart,
     Spread into my heart, Lord Jesus;
     Make home today and have Your way
     In all of my heart, Lord Jesus.

2   Spread into my heart, O Lord Jesus,
     Spread into my heart, I pray;
     Spread into my heart from my spirit,
     Spread into my heart today.

3   Make home in my heart, O Lord Jesus,
     Make home in my heart, I pray;
     That we may be filled with Your fullness,
     Make home in my heart today.

4   To Him who is able to do it
     Above all we think or say,
     We open our hearts wide and welcome
     Him into our heart today.

Composition for prophecy with main point and sub-points: _____

_____

_____

_____

_____

_____

_____

_____

_____

_____

_____

_____

_____

_____

_____

_____

_____

_____

_____

_____

_____

_____

_____

_____

_____

_____

_____

_____

_____

_____

_____

_____

_____

_____

_____

_____

Knowing the Significance
of Loving the Lord,
Loving the Lord Jesus Christ
in Incorruptibility,
and Walking in Love and Light

Scripture Reading: Mark 12:30; 1 Cor. 2:9; 2 Tim. 4:8; Eph.
6:24; 5:1-14

Day 1 **I. We need to know the significance of loving the Lord (Mark 12:30; 1 Cor. 2:9):**

A. To love the Lord is to allow Him to live in us and for us and is to realize that He desires a dwelling place so that He can be expressed (Eph. 3:16-17).

B. Our believing into the Lord is for our receiving Him, and our loving Him is for our enjoying Him (Titus 3:15).

C. To love the Lord is to be stopped from our doing and is to let Him take full possession of our being (Eph. 3:16-19; Gal. 4:19).

D. The best way to express our love toward the Lord is to say, "Lord Jesus, I open to You. Take full possession of me. Lord, I love You. I present myself to You. I am open to You. Possess me more and more until You reach every part of my being and make Your home in me."

Day 2 E. According to 1 Corinthians, in order to love the Lord, we need to take Him as our portion for our enjoyment (1:2, 9; 5:7-8; 10:3-4), allow Him to grow in us (3:6), and realize that we are one spirit with Him (6:17).

F. We love the Lord by being fully occupied by Him and loving His appearing (2 Tim. 4:8):

1. To be a lover of God is to be fully occupied, possessed, and taken over by God (Eph. 3:16-19; Gal. 4:19).

2. If we love the Lord in this way, we will love His appearing (2 Tim. 4:8):

a. According to Paul's word, a crown is laid up for those who love the Lord's appearing (v. 8).

b. If we do not love the Lord, His coming will be a matter of judgment (1 Cor. 16:22), but if we love Him and His appearing, we will receive a prize.

II. **"Grace be with all those who love our Lord Jesus Christ in incorruptibility" (Eph. 6:24):**

A. According to the usage of *incorruptible* in the writings of Paul, this word refers mainly to God and the things of God; everything natural is corruptible, but God, the divine life, and all things that are in resurrection are incorruptible (1 Tim. 1:17; 2 Tim. 1:10; 1 Cor. 15:42, 52-54).

B. To love our Lord Jesus Christ in incorruptibility means to love Him in the new creation and according to all the incorruptible things revealed in Ephesians:

1. We need to love the Lord Jesus in His being the embodiment of the Triune God (Col. 2:9); in His being the element of the Body (1 Cor. 12:12); in His being reality, grace, peace, love, and light (John 1:17; 8:12; 14:6, 27; 1 John 4:8); and in His being the constituent of the one new man (Eph. 2:15; Col. 3:10-11).

2. All these things are related to what is revealed in and taught in Ephesians, including the Triune God, Christ, and His Body, the church.

3. Ephesians speaks concerning the dispensing of the Triune God to produce the church (1:3-23; 3:16-21), concerning what Christ is and has done for the church (1:7; 2:13-18; 5:25-27, 29), and concerning the church being the Body of Christ, being the bride of Christ, and being one with Christ in the heavenlies (1:22-23; 5:23, 25-27; 2:6).

4. All these matters are incorruptible, and we need to love the Lord in these incorruptible

things:

Day 3

    a. If we love the Lord Jesus in all these things, our love toward Him will be incorruptible (6:24).

    b. Such a love is not a natural love—it is a love in resurrection, the love that God Himself is in His divine essence (1 John 4:16).

C. In the Lord's recovery we need to love our Lord Jesus Christ in all the divine, spiritual, heavenly, and incorruptible things revealed in Ephesians concerning the Triune God, the divine life, what Christ is to us, what He has done, and the church (1:3-23; 2:5-6, 13-18; 3:16-21; 4:4-6; 5:23, 25-27).

III. **The more we love the Lord in incorruptibility, the more we, as children of God, will walk in love and light (vv. 1-14):**

A. As the children of God, we are God-men, born of God, possessing the life and nature of God, and belonging to the species of God (v. 1; 1 John 3:1; John 1:12-13):

    1. God is our real, genuine, Father, and we are His real, genuine, children (1 John 3:1; Eph. 5:1).

    2. The greatest wonder in the universe is that human beings could be begotten of God and that sinners could be made children of God (1 John 3:1, 9; 4:7; 5:1, 4, 18; John 1:12-13):

        a. Since we have been born of the divine life and possess the divine life, we, the children of God, are divine persons (1 John 5:11-13; 3:1, 10).

        b. As those who have been born of God, we have not only the divine life but also the divine nature (2 Pet. 1:4).

Day 4

B. As the children of God, we should walk in love and light (Eph. 5:2, 8):

    1. Love is the inner substance of God, and light is the expressed element of God (1 John 4:8, 16; 1:5).

2. Our daily walk as children of God should be constituted with both the loving substance of God and the shining element of God; this should be the inner source of our walk (Eph. 5:2, 8).

3. "Walk in love, even as Christ also loved us and gave Himself up for us, an offering and a sacrifice to God for a sweet-smelling savor" (v. 2):

   a. The goal of the book of Ephesians is to bring us into love as the inner substance of God so that we may enjoy His presence in the sweetness of the divine love and thereby love others as Christ did (v. 25):

      (1) In the condition and atmosphere of love, we are saturated with God to be holy and without blemish before Him (1:4).

      (2) The love in which we are rooted for growth and grounded for building is the divine love realized and experienced by us in a practical way (3:17).

      (3) The love of Christ, which is Christ Himself, is immeasurable and knowledge-surpassing, yet we can know it by experiencing it (v. 19).

      (4) The Body of Christ builds itself up in love; love is the most excellent way for us to be anything and to do anything for the building up of the Body of Christ (4:16; 1 Cor. 12:31).

   b. As those who have been regenerated to become God's species, we, the children of God, should be love because God is love; since we become God in life and in nature, we also should become love (1 John 4:8, 16).

4. "You were once darkness but are now light in the Lord; walk as children of light" (Eph. 5:8):

   a. As God is light, so we, the children of God,

Day 5

are children of light (1 John 1:5; Eph. 5:8; John 12:36).

b. We are not only children of light—we are light itself; we are light because we are one with God in the Lord (Matt. 5:14; 1 John 1:5).

Day 6

c. When we are in the light, we are outside the realm of right and wrong (v. 7).

d. If we walk as children of light, we will bear the fruit described in Ephesians 5:9:

(1) The fruit of the light must be good in nature, righteous in procedure, and real in expression, that God may be expressed as the reality of our daily walk.

(2) The fruit of the light in goodness, righteousness, and truth is related to the Triune God:

(a) God the Father as goodness is the nature of the fruit of the light; therefore, goodness in verse 9 refers to God the Father (Matt. 19:17).

(b) Righteousness refers to God the Son, for Christ came to accomplish God's purpose according to God's righteous procedure (Rom. 5:17-18, 21).

(c) Truth, the expression of the fruit of the light, refers to God the Spirit, for He is the Spirit of reality (John 14:17; 16:13).

(d) The proof that we are walking as children of light is seen in the bearing of such fruit.

Morning Nourishment

Mark "And you shall love the Lord your God from your
12:30 whole heart and from your whole soul and from
your whole mind and from your whole strength."

1 Cor. But as it is written, "Things which eye has not seen
2:9 and ear has not heard and *which* have not come up
in man's heart; things which God has prepared for
those who love Him."

We need to see that to love the Lord is to allow Him to live
in us and for us. He desires a dwelling place and a vessel so
that He can be expressed. If we sincerely love the Lord, we
need to say, "Lord Jesus, I stop all my doing and give You the
free way to live in me and to live for me." (*CWWL, 1973-1974,*
vol. 2, p. 453)

Today's Reading

The Gospel of John reveals that God became a man in
order to present Himself to man (1:1, 14). As a man He asked
us to do two things—first to receive Him into us by believing
into Him and second to love Him (v. 12; 14:21, 23; 21:15-17).
Our believing into the Lord is for our receiving Him, and our
loving Him is for our enjoying Him. Receiving and enjoying
are not the same thing. We receive food when we buy groceries,
but we must prepare and eat the food in order to enjoy it.
Every believer has received the Lord. Although we have already
received Him, we still need to love Him. We should tell
the Lord that we love Him every day, morning and evening. It
is good to pray each morning, "Lord, I still love You. I love You
more today than yesterday." Throughout the day, although we
may not have a burden to pray for anything in particular, we
should often pray, "Lord Jesus, I love You. I still love You. I love
You more than ever. You are so lovable." No other kind of
prayer will stir us up as much as telling the Lord that we love
Him. After the day has passed, when we get into bed, we
should say, "Lord Jesus, now that this day has passed, I tell
You that I still love You. I love You. I love You more than

anything." The more we tell the Lord that we love Him, the more He will show us how lovely He is until we realize that He is altogether lovely.

Believing into the Lord and loving Him are the two basic requirements for us to participate in His riches. We must first receive Him into us and then love Him continually.

To love the Lord is not to do good things or even spiritual things. Instead, to love the Lord is to be stopped from our doing and to let the Lord take full possession of our being. We need to pray, "It is no longer I who live, but it is Christ who lives in me. Lord, live in me and live for me. I repent that for many years I have not given You the opportunity to live in me and for me. Now I see that I need to love You, give myself to You, and let You have all the ground in me and a free course to live in me and for me."

The best way to express our love toward the Lord is to say, "Lord Jesus, I open to You. Take full possession of me." Rather than needing us to do something for Him, the Lord needs us to be His dwelling place to express Him. He wants us to open to Him so that He can make His home in our heart. In order to properly express our love toward the Lord, we must stop any kind of doing based on good intentions, such as being a proper spouse or bringing many to salvation.

We need to stop our doing so that it is no longer we who live. We have been crucified, and a crucified person cannot do anything. Not only should we no longer do bad things, but we also should no longer do good things from ourselves. If we do anything, it means that we are not crucified. The way to love the Lord is not to try to do anything but simply to say, "Lord, I love You. I present myself to You. I am open to You. Possess me more and more until You reach every part of my being and make Your home in me." (*CWWL, 1973-1974,* vol. 2, pp. 446-447, 453, 451-452)

Further Reading: CWWL, 1973-1974, vol. 2, pp. 445-453

Enlightenment and inspiration: _____

_____

_____

_____

Morning Nourishment

2 Tim. Henceforth there is laid up for me the crown of
4:8 righteousness, with which the Lord, the righteous
Judge, will recompense me in that day, and not only
me but also all those who have loved His appearing.
Eph. Grace be with all those who love our Lord Jesus
6:24 Christ in incorruptibility.

First Corinthians reveals how to love the Lord. In this Epistle the apostle Paul does not tell us to do many things, such as go to the mission field or give everything to the Lord. According to 1 Corinthians, in order to love the Lord, we first need to take Him as our portion for our enjoyment (1:2, 9; 5:7-8; 10:3-4). We need to say, "Lord, You are my portion. You are edible and drinkable. You are my enjoyment." Second, to love the Lord is to allow Him to grow in us (3:6). We need not only to enjoy Him but also to let Him continually increase in our being. Third, in order to love the Lord, we need to realize that we are one spirit with Him (6:17). Instead of doing things for the Lord, such as exercising spiritual gifts or going to the mission field, we mainly need to pray, "Lord, You are my enjoyment, You are growing within me, and You and I are one spirit. In every aspect of my daily life I enjoy oneness with You in my spirit." This is to love the Lord. (*CWWL, 1973-1974,* vol. 2, p. 452)

Today's Reading

In 2 Timothy Paul says, "In the last days difficult times will come. For men will be lovers of self, lovers of money,…lovers of pleasure rather than lovers of God" (3:1-2, 4). To be a lover of money is to be fully occupied, possessed, and taken over by money, even dreaming of money. Similarly, to be a lover of God is to be fully occupied, possessed, and taken over by God. In the United States people have many pleasures, such as sports and other amusements. A lover of sports is fully occupied by sports. To love the Lord is to be fully occupied by Him. Even in our dreams we should say, "Lord Jesus, I love You."

If we love the Lord in this way, we will love His appearing, which is His coming. Paul says, "Henceforth there is laid up for me the crown of righteousness, with which the Lord, the righteous Judge, will recompense me in that day, and not only me but also all those who have loved His appearing" (4:8). We should pray, "Lord, although I have given You a free course to live in me and for me, I still long for Your outward appearing. Come quickly, Lord Jesus!" According to Paul's word, a crown is laid up for those who love the Lord's appearing. If we do not love the Lord, His coming will be a matter of judgment (1 Cor. 16:22), but if we love Him and His appearing, we will receive a prize. (*CWWL, 1973-1974,* vol. 2, pp. 452-453)

Ephesians 6:24 says, "Grace be with all those who love our Lord Jesus Christ in incorruptibility."...Everything natural is corruptible, but God, the divine life, and all things that are in resurrection are incorruptible (1 Tim. 1:17; 2 Tim. 1:10; 1 Cor. 15:42, 52-54). According to the usage of *incorruptible,* especially in the writings of Paul, this word refers mainly to God and the things of God. We need to love the Lord Jesus in His being the embodiment of the Triune God (Col. 2:9); in His being the element of the Body (1 Cor. 12:12); in His being reality, grace, peace, love, and light (John 1:17; 8:12; 14:6; Eph. 2:14; 1 John 4:8); and in His being the constituent of the new man (Eph. 2:15; Col. 3:10-11). All these things are related to what is revealed and taught in Ephesians, including the Triune God, Christ, and His Body, the church. Ephesians speaks concerning the dispensing of the Triune God to produce the church (1:3-23; 3:16-21), and it speaks of what Christ is and has done for the church. It also speaks about the church being the Body of Christ, being the bride of Christ, and being one with Christ in the heavenlies (1:22-23; 5:23, 25-27; 2:6). All these matters are incorruptible. We need to love Christ in these incorruptible things.

To love the Lord Jesus in all the above matters is to love Him in incorruptibility. (*CWWL, 1991-1992,* vol. 1, p. 67)

Further Reading: CWWL, 1988, vol. 1, pp. 551-556

Enlightenment and inspiration: _____

_____

_____

_____

Morning Nourishment

John
1:12
But as many as received Him, to them He gave the authority to become children of God, to those who believe into His name.

2 Pet.
1:4
Through which He has granted to us precious and exceedingly great promises that through these you might become partakers of the divine nature, having escaped the corruption which is in the world by lust.

In the past, many thousands of believers have loved Christ. Some have loved the Lord Jesus because He is kind to them, because He cares for them, because of what He has given them, or simply because He first loved them. According to Paul's word, however, we must love the Lord Jesus in all the items unveiled in Ephesians. Every chapter unveils something concerning Christ and His Body, the church. If we love Him in all these things, our love toward Him will be incorruptible. Such love is not a natural love. It is a love in resurrection, the love that is God Himself in His divine essence (1 John 4:16). I hope that in the Lord's recovery we would all love the Lord Jesus Christ not in many other things but in all the divine, spiritual, heavenly, and incorruptible things revealed in Ephesians concerning the Triune God, the divine life, what Christ is to us, what He has done, and the church. (*CWWL, 1991-1992,* vol. 1, pp. 67-68)

Today's Reading

John 3:6 says, "That which is born of the flesh is flesh." Both you and your parents are of the same species, the species of flesh. Verse 6 also says, "That which is born of the Spirit is spirit." The two spirits are of the same species and also of the same source. We are born of God to be the many God-men, the children of God.

Adam was the son of God in image and likeness, but he had only the image of God without the life and nature of God. We are different. We are not only created by God but also born of God, so God is our real, genuine, Father, and we are His real, genuine, children. We have the authority to say that we are children of God. We have God's image and His life and nature. Romans 8:16 says that the

Spirit and our spirit witness together that we are children of God....The children of God are the God-men. When we received the Lord Jesus and He came into our spirit, right away an authority was given to us. That authority was the divine life, and with this life is the divine nature. We have the life and nature of God because we were born of God to be His children. We are God-men. (*CWWL, 1994-1997,* vol. 3, "The God-man Living," pp. 461-462)

We have been begotten of the Father, the source of life, to be the children of God. Surely it is the greatest wonder in the universe that human beings could be begotten of God and sinners could be made children of God. Through such an amazing divine birth we have received the divine life, the eternal life. (*The Conclusion of the New Testament,* p. 1071)

As sons of God and as God-men, we have the divine life (John 3:15, 36a). Many Christians realize that they have eternal life, yet they do not know what eternal life is. Furthermore, they do not know what the divine life is. They do not know that, as regenerated ones, they have another life in addition to their own human life. We all need to realize that in addition to our natural life, we have another life, the divine life. The natural life makes us a natural man, and the divine life makes us a divine man. We all can boast that we are divine persons because we have been born of the divine life. Since we have been born of the divine life and possess the divine life, surely we are divine persons. We have been born of the divine life; therefore, we are divine.

As those who are born of God, the God-men have not only the divine life but also the divine nature. Thank God that in the Bible, among the sixty-six books, there is one verse, 2 Peter 1:4, that says that we are partakers of the divine nature, which is the nature of God. We should mark such a verse in our Bibles so that whenever we open the Bible, that verse will stand out. (*CWWL, 1994-1997,* vol. 2, "The God-men," pp. 437-438)

Further Reading: CWWL, 1985, vol. 3, "Elders' Training, Book 6: The Crucial Points of the Truth in Paul's Epistles," pp. 517-519

Enlightenment and inspiration: _____

_____

_____

_____

Morning Nourishment

Eph. **And walk in love, even as Christ also loved us and**
5:2   **gave Himself up for us, an offering and a sacrifice**
      to God for a sweet-smelling savor.
1 John **And we know and have believed the love which**
4:16 **God has in us. God is love, and he who abides in**
      love abides in God and God abides in him.

According to Ephesians 4, we need grace and truth for the life
that qualifies us to participate in the building up of the Body of
Christ. Chapter 5 of Ephesians is higher and deeper than chapter 4. It goes on to show us that we need to walk in love and light
(5:2, 8). Love is the source of grace, and light is the source of truth.
When love is expressed, it becomes grace. When light shines out,
it becomes truth. Christ came from God to express God, to manifest God. When God is expressed and revealed in the Lord Jesus,
His love becomes grace and His light becomes truth. When we
receive the Lord Jesus as our Savior and our life, we are brought
into fellowship with the Father to enjoy Him as love and light.
(*CWWL, 1988,* vol. 3, "The Body of Christ," pp. 412-413)

Today's Reading

The Son is the expression of love, which to us is grace, and
this grace brings us to the source of grace, which is the Father
as love. In the Gospel of John there is grace (1:14), but in the
first Epistle of John there is love (4:8, 16). Christ also came to
bring us the truth, the reality. When we have the truth, the
truth brings us to the source of truth, the Father as light. Jesus
Christ brings us to the Father, who is love as the source of grace
and who is light as the source of truth. In Ephesians 5 we are
children of light walking in love and light. (*CWWL, 1988,* vol. 3,
"The Body of Christ," p. 413)

Love is the inner substance of God, whereas light is the
expressed element of God. The inward love of God is sensible,
and the outward light of God is visible. Our walk in love should
be constituted of both the loving substance and the shining element of God. These should be the inner source of our walk.

They are deeper than grace and truth. (Eph. 5:2, footnote 1)

May we all be impressed that the church life according to God's desire must be in love and in light, both of which are the very elements of God Himself. In the inner substance of God we have love and light. Here we have the top church life, the church as the bride. The goal of the book of Ephesians is to bring us into God's inner substance to know Him as love and light. Here we are to live in intimate fellowship as we enjoy the shining light and love in its sweetness.

We shall be holy and without blemish before Him in love. Love here refers to the love with which God loves His chosen ones and with which His chosen ones love Him. It is in this love, in such a love, that God's chosen ones become holy and without blemish before Him. Firstly, God loved us. Then this divine love inspires us to love Him in return. In such a condition and atmosphere of love, we are saturated with God to be holy and without blemish as He is. In this love, a mutual love, God loves us, and we return this love to Him. It is in this kind of condition that we are being transformed. Under such a condition we are being saturated with God.

Paul says specifically that we are rooted and grounded in *love*. In order to experience Christ, we need faith and love (1 Tim. 1:14). Faith enables us to receive and realize Christ, and love enables us to enjoy Him. Both faith and love are not ours but His. His faith becomes our faith to believe in Him, and His love becomes our love to love Him. The love in which we are rooted and grounded is the divine love realized and experienced by us in a practical way. With such a love we love the Lord, and with that same love we love one another. In such a love we grow in life and are built up in life. Paul's thought here regarding the relationship between the experience of Christ and the matters of life and building is surely deep and profound. (*Life-study of Ephesians,* pp. 516, 32-33, 289-290)

Further Reading: Life-study of Ephesians, msgs. 33, 61

Enlightenment and inspiration: _____

_____

_____

_____

Morning Nourishment

Eph. And to know the knowledge-surpassing love of
3:19 Christ, that you may be filled unto all the fullness
of God.
4:16 Out from whom all the Body, being joined together
and being knit together through every joint of the
rich supply and *through* the operation in the measure of each one part, causes the growth of the Body
unto the building up of itself in love.

The love of Christ surpasses knowledge; yet, we can know
it by experiencing it. According to our mentality, the love of
Christ is knowledge-surpassing. Our mind is not able to know
it. But in our spirit we can know the love of Christ through our
experience.

The love of Christ is Christ Himself. Just as Christ is immeasurable, so His love is also immeasurable. Do not regard the love
of Christ as something belonging to Christ. This love *is* Christ.
Because Christ is immeasurable, His love is knowledge-surpassing; yet we can know it in our spirit, not by knowledge but
by experience. If we compare what we have so far experienced of
the immeasurable love of Christ to all there is to experience, it is
like comparing a raindrop to the ocean. Christ in His universal
dimensions and in His immeasurable love is like a vast, limitless
ocean for us to experience. (*Life-study of Ephesians,* p. 290)

Today's Reading

The end of 1 Corinthians 12 reveals that love is the most excellent way (v. 31b). How can one be an elder? Love is the most
excellent way. How can one be a co-worker? Love is the most excellent way. How do we shepherd people? Love is the most excellent way. Love is the most excellent way for us to prophesy and to
teach others. Love is the most excellent way for us to be anything
or do anything.

Love prevails. We should love everybody, even our enemies. If
the co-workers and elders do not love the bad ones, eventually
they will have nothing to do. We must be perfect as our Father is

perfect (Matt. 5:48) by loving the evil ones and the good ones without any discrimination. We must be perfect as our Father because we are His sons, His species. This is most crucial. How can we be a co-worker and an elder? It is by love in every way. We must love any kind of person. (*CWWL, 1994-1997,* vol. 5, "The Vital Groups," p. 126)

Because God is love as well as Spirit, the more we are under His dispensing, the more love we have. Actually, the more God's nature is dispensed into us, the more we become love. This means that we not only have love but that we are love. When the New Testament says that God is love, this does not mean that God merely has love but that He is love. Through God's dispensing of Himself into us, we become love in the sense of being constituted of God as love. When love as the nature of God's essence is dispensed into us, we shall react to others in love. Only one kind of love is genuine, and that is the love that comes out of God's dispensing. When we are under God's dispensing, we react with genuine love, which is God Himself.

When we are under God's dispensing, our living will not only be with Spirit and love but also with light. Our natural love is in darkness. Only one kind of love is full of light, and that is the love that comes from God's dispensing. (*The Conclusion of the New Testament,* p. 70)

In Ephesians 5:8 Paul says, "For you were once darkness but are now light in the Lord; walk as children of light." We were once not only dark, but darkness itself. Now we are not only the children of light, but light itself (Matt. 5:14). As light is God, so darkness is the devil. We were darkness because we were one with the devil. Now we are light because we are one with God in the Lord.

In Ephesians 5:8 Paul exhorts us to "walk as children of light." As God is light, so we, the children of God, are also the children of light. Because we are now light in the Lord, we should walk as children of light. (*Life-study of Ephesians,* p. 425)

Further Reading: CWWL, 1994-1997, vol. 5, "The Vital Groups," ch. 8

Enlightenment and inspiration: _____

_____

_____

_____

Morning Nourishment

1 John   But if we walk in the light as He is in the light, we
1:7   have fellowship with one another, and the blood of
         Jesus His Son cleanses us from every sin.

Eph.   For you were once darkness but are now light in
5:8-9   the Lord; walk as children of light (for the fruit
         of the light *consists* in all goodness and righteous-
         ness and truth).

Although it is rather easy to understand the difference between love and grace, it is more difficult to understand the dis-
tinction between light and truth. Perhaps it will help if I illustrate
from my own experience in married life. My wife and I have been
married for a good many years. During this time, I cannot recall
ever dealing with her according to what I thought was right. On
the contrary, by the Lord's enabling, I have behaved toward her
always in light. When we are in the light, we are outside the realm
of right and wrong. There is no need to discern what is right and
what is wrong, what we should do and what we should not do. If
we are in the light, we simply act and behave spontaneously in a
certain way. However, when we are in darkness, we need to discern, to guess, and to grope for a way to do things. But when we
are in the light, there is no need for groping, guessing, or discerning. (*Life-study of Ephesians*, pp. 511-512)

Today's Reading

After commanding us to walk as children of light, Paul
inserts in Ephesians 5:9 a parenthetical statement regarding
the fruit of the light, saying that "the fruit of the light consists
in all goodness and righteousness and truth." Goodness is the
nature of the fruit of the light; righteousness is the way or the
procedure to produce the fruit of the light; and the truth is the
reality, the real expression of the fruit of the light. This expression is God Himself. The fruit of the light must be good in
nature, righteous in procedure, and real in expression so that
God may be expressed as the reality of our daily walk.

It is significant that in speaking of the fruit of the light Paul mentions only three things: goodness, righteousness, and truth. He does not speak of holiness, kindness, or humility. The reason he mentions just three things is that the fruit of the light in goodness, righteousness, and truth is related to the Triune God. Goodness refers to the nature of the fruit of light. The Lord Jesus once indicated that the only One who is good is God Himself (Matt. 19:17). Hence, goodness here denotes God the Father. God the Father as goodness is the nature of the fruit of the light.

Notice that here Paul speaks not of the work of the light nor of the conduct of the light, but of the fruit of the light. Fruit is a matter of life with its nature. The nature of the fruit of the light is God the Father.

We have pointed out that the righteousness denotes the way or the procedure of the fruit of the light. Righteousness is the procedure by which the fruit of the light is produced. In the Godhead, the Son, Christ, is our righteousness. He came to earth to produce certain things according to God's procedure, which is always righteous. Righteousness is God's way, God's procedure. Christ came to accomplish God's purpose according to His righteous procedure. Therefore, the second aspect of the fruit of the light refers to God the Son.

The truth is the expression of the fruit of the light. This fruit must be real; that is, it must be the expression of God, the shining of the hidden light. No doubt, this truth refers to the Spirit of reality, the third of the Triune God. Therefore, the Father as the goodness, the Son as the righteousness, and the Spirit as the truth, the reality, are all related to the fruit of the light.

Ephesians 5:9 is the definition of walking as children of light. If we walk as the children of light, we shall bear the fruit described in verse 9. The fruit we bear by walking as the children of the light must be in goodness, in righteousness, and in truth. The proof that we are walking as children of light is seen in the bearing of such fruit. (*Life-study of Ephesians,* pp. 426-428)

Further Reading: Life-study of Ephesians, msg. 50

Enlightenment and inspiration: _____

_____

_____

_____

Hymns, #13

1 Thou art love and Thou art light, Lord,
In the Son as life Thou art;
Love expressing, light illum'ning,
Thou dost life to us impart.

Thou art love! Thou art light!
In the Son as life Thou art;
Love expressing, light illum'ning,
Thou dost life to us impart.

2 Love bespeaks Thy very being,
What Thou dost is shown by light;
Love is inward, light is outward,
Love accompanies the light.

3 Love by grace is manifested,
And the light by truth is shown;
By Thy love we may enjoy Thee;
By Thy light Thou, Lord, art known.

4 Through Thy love, which led to Calvary,
We receive the life of God;
Light our understanding opens,
That we may apply the blood.

5 Through Thy love, as life Thou enter'st
Fellowship with Thee to give;
Through Thy light we take Thy cleansing
And in fellowship may live.

6 By the light and blood which cleanses,
The anointing we shall know;
Then the life of love Thine essence,
More and more in us will flow.

7 By Thy love we are Thy children,
Abba Father calling Thee;
Light disperses all our darkness,
Till, like Him, Thy Son, we see.

Oh, what grace! Oh, what truth!
Love is seen and light is shown!
We would praise Thee never ceasing,
Thou by love and light art known!

Composition for prophecy with main point and sub-points: _____

_____
_____
_____
_____
_____
_____
_____
_____
_____
_____
_____
_____
_____
_____
_____
_____
_____
_____
_____
_____
_____
_____
_____
_____
_____
_____
_____
_____
_____
_____
_____
_____
_____
_____
_____
_____
_____
_____
_____

The Apostolic Ministry in Cooperation
with Christ's Heavenly Ministry

Scripture Reading: John 21:15-17; 10:10-11, 16; Acts 20:20,
31; 1 Pet. 2:25; 5:1-4; Heb. 13:20-21

Day 1   I. **John 21 is the completion and consummation**
of the Gospel of John:
A. The Gospel of John has twenty-one chapters, but
it actually ends with chapter 20; the entire book
covers the earthly ministry of Christ, beginning
with His incarnation as the Word of God to become a man in the flesh (1:1, 14) and ending with
His resurrection as the last Adam to become the
life-giving Spirit (20:22; 1 Cor. 15:45b); hence,
John 21 should be an appendix.
B. Although it is correct to say this, it is more intrinsic to say that John 21 is the completion and consummation of the Gospel of John; chapter 21
consummates the entire Gospel of John by showing that Christ's heavenly ministry and the apostles' ministry on the earth cooperate together to
carry out God's New Testament economy.
   II. **In 10:10, 11, and 16 the Lord unveiled to the**
disciples that He was the good Shepherd who
came that the sheep might have life abun-
dantly and that He had other sheep (the
Gentiles) that He must lead to join with them
(the Jewish believers) to be one flock (one
church) under one Shepherd:
A. First, the Lord's shepherding was in His earthly
ministry (Matt. 9:36; 10:1-6).
B. Second, the Lord's shepherding is in His heavenly ministry (1 Pet. 5:4) to take care of the
church, issuing in His Body.
  III. **In this appendix, when the Lord stayed with**
His disciples after His resurrection and be-
fore His ascension, in one of His appearings,
He commissioned Peter to feed His lambs

**and shepherd His sheep in His absence, while
He is in the heavens (John 21:15-17):**

A. This is to incorporate the apostolic ministry
with Christ's heavenly ministry to take care of
God's flock, which is the church that issues in
the Body of Christ.

B. The following words of the apostle Paul confirm
this:

1. "Take heed to yourselves and to all the flock,
among whom the Holy Spirit has placed
you as overseers to shepherd the church of
God, which He obtained through His own
blood" (Acts 20:28).

2. "Fierce wolves will come in among you, not
sparing the flock" (v. 29).

3. "God...brought up from the dead our Lord
Jesus, the great Shepherd of the sheep, in the
blood of an eternal covenant" (Heb. 13:20).

Day 2 **IV. Peter was so impressed with this commission of the Lord that:**

A. In his first book he tells the believers that they
were like sheep being led astray, but they have
now returned to the Shepherd and Overseer
(Christ) of their souls (1 Pet. 2:25).

B. He exhorts the elders to shepherd the flock of
God among them so that when the Chief Shepherd is manifested, they will receive the unfad-
ing crown of glory (5:1-4).

C. Peter tells the elders that their obligation is to
shepherd God's flock according to God (vv. 1-2):

1. *According to God* means that we must live
God; we must have God on hand.

2. When we are one with God, we become God
in life and in nature but not in the Godhead;
then we have God and are the acting God in
our shepherding of others.

3. To shepherd according to God is to shepherd
according to what God is in His attributes—
love, light, holiness, and righteousness.

4. To shepherd according to God is to shepherd according to God's nature, desire, way, and glory, not according to man's preference, interest, and purpose.

D. Peter's word indicates that the heavenly ministry of Christ is mainly to shepherd the church of God as His flock, which issues in His Body.

V. **The main purpose and goal of the apostolic ministry incorporated with Christ's heavenly ministry are to build up the Body of Christ, which will consummate the New Jerusalem for the accomplishment of the eternal economy of God.**

VI. **The matter of shepherding God's flock for the main purpose and ultimate consummation of the eternal economy of God is referred to even in Song of Songs:**

A. "Tell me, you whom my soul loves, Where do you pasture your flock [for satisfaction]? / Where do you make it lie down at noon [for rest]?" (1:7a).

B. "Go forth on the footsteps of the flock, / And pasture your young goats / By the shepherds' tents" (v. 8b).

C. "My beloved is mine, and I am his; / He pastures his flock among the lilies [the seekers of Christ who live a life of trusting in God with a single heart]" (2:16).

D. "I am my beloved's, and my beloved is mine; / He pastures his flock among the lilies" (6:3).

Day 3 VII. **Without John 21 as such an appendix, the Gospel of John does not have an adequate and complete ending:**

A. If we do not know what shepherding is, the entire Gospel of John will be in vain to us; it is only when we shepherd others that we can know John in an intrinsic way; shepherding is the key to the Gospel of John.

B. We must take the shepherding way to preach the gospel and revive the church:

1. We must not lord it over God's allotments but become patterns of the flock (1 Pet. 5:3).
2. We must be willing to be slaves to the saints and must humble ourselves under the saints.
3. The elders should shepherd one another and love one another to be a model of the Body life.
4. We must take care of the saints in everything and in every way for the dispensing of Christ into them.
5. We must contact and visit the saints and invite them to our home for meals.

VIII. **We need to shepherd people according to the pattern of the Lord Jesus in His ministry for carrying out God's eternal economy (Matt. 9:36; John 10:11):**

Day 4 A. In Luke 15 the Lord Jesus unveiled the saving love of the Triune God for sinners:
1. We need to follow the steps of the processed Triune God in seeking and gaining fallen people (vv. 1-10, 17-18).
2. Our not having the Father's loving and forgiving heart and the Savior's shepherding and seeking spirit is the reason for our barrenness.
3. We need to cherish people (to make them happy and to make them feel pleasant and comfortable) in the humanity of Jesus (Matt. 9:10; Luke 7:34).
4. We need to nourish people (to feed them with the all-inclusive Christ in His ministry of three stages) in the divinity of Christ (Matt. 24:45-47).

B. Christ came not as a Judge but as a Physician to heal, recover, enliven, and save the lepers (8:2-4), paralytics (vv. 5-13; 9:2-8), the fever-ridden (8:14-15), the demon-possessed (vv. 16, 28-32), those ill with all kinds of diseases (v. 16), despised tax collectors, and sinners (9:9-11) that they might be reconstituted to become people of His heavenly kingdom (vv. 12-13).

Day 5

C. He had to pass through Samaria, purposely detouring to Sychar to gain one immoral woman, cherishing her by asking her to give Him something to drink that He might nourish her with the flowing Triune God as the water of life (John 4:3-14).

D. As the One without sin, He did not condemn the adulterous woman but cherished her by forgiving her sins judicially and setting her free from her sins organically (8:1-11, 32, 36).

E. He went to Jericho just to visit and gain one person, a chief tax collector, and His preaching was a shepherding (Luke 19:1-10).

F. He cherished the parents by laying His hands on their children (Matt. 19:13-15).

G. The first one saved by Christ through His crucifixion was a robber sentenced to death (Luke 23:42-43).

H. In His heavenly ministry Christ as the High Priest, with a golden girdle about His breasts, is cherishing and nourishing the churches (Rev. 1:12-13).

I. In His heavenly ministry Christ is the great Shepherd of the sheep to consummate the New Jerusalem according to God's eternal covenant (Heb. 13:20-21).

IX. **The apostles were a pattern of the glad tidings that they spread—"you know what kind of men we were among you for your sake" (1 Thes. 1:5b):**

A. In the church the most important thing is the person; the person is the way, and the person is the Lord's work; what you are is what you do (John 5:19; 6:57; Phil. 1:19-26; Acts 20:18-35; Matt. 7:17-18; 12:33-37).

B. We need to follow the pattern of the apostles to pay more attention to life than to work (John

12:24; 2 Cor. 4:12).

C. Paul shepherded the saints as a nursing mother and an exhorting father (1 Thes. 2:7-8, 11-12).

D. Paul shepherded the saints in Ephesus by teaching them "publicly and from house to house" (Acts 20:20) and by admonishing each one of the saints with tears even for as long as three years (vv. 31, 19), declaring to them all the counsel of God (v. 27).

E. He had an intimate concern for the believers (2 Cor. 7:3; Philem. 7, 12).

F. He came down to the weak ones' level so that he could gain them (2 Cor. 11:28-29; 1 Cor. 9:22; cf. Matt. 12:20).

G. He was willing to spend what he had, referring to his possessions, and to spend what he was, referring to his being, for the sake of the saints (2 Cor. 12:15).

H. He was a drink offering, one with Christ as the wine producer, sacrificing himself for others' enjoyment of Christ (Phil. 2:17; Judg. 9:13; Eph. 3:2).

I. Paul indicated in his teaching that the church is a home to raise up people, a hospital to heal and recover them, and a school to teach and edify them (2:19; 1 Thes. 5:14; 1 Cor. 14:31).

X. **"I hope that there will be a genuine revival among us by our receiving this burden of shepherding. If all the churches receive this teaching to participate in Christ's wonderful shepherding, there will be a big revival in the recovery"** (*The Vital Groups*, **p. 40**) **(cf. Psa. 22—24 [footnote 1 on 22:1 and footnote 1 on 24:1]).**

Morning Nourishment

John
21:15-17

...Jesus said to Simon Peter,...Do you love Me...? He said to Him, Yes, Lord, You know that I love You. He said to him, Feed My lambs. He said to him again a second time,...Do you love Me? He said to Him, Yes, Lord, You know that I love You. He said to him, Shepherd My sheep. He said to him the third time,...Do you love Me?...And he said to Him, Lord,...You know that I love You. Jesus said to him, Feed My sheep.

John 21 reveals the apostolic ministry in cooperation with Christ's heavenly ministry. After Christ ascended to the heavens, He began His heavenly ministry. In doing this, He raised up a group of His followers as His apostles who could fully cooperate with Him. These apostles were commissioned by the ascended Christ to cooperate with Him to carry out God's New Testament economy. What He was doing in the heavens, the apostles did on earth to carry out His heavenly ministry. (*CWWL, 1994-1997,* vol. 4, "Crystallization-study of the Gospel of John," p. 446)

Today's Reading

The entire [Gospel of John] covers the earthly ministry of Christ, beginning with His incarnation as the Word of God to become a man in the flesh (1:1-14) and ending with His resurrection as the last Adam to become the life-giving Spirit (ch. 20); hence, chapter 21 should be an appendix. Although it is correct to say this, it is more intrinsic to say that John 21 is the completion and consummation of the Gospel of John....[This chapter] consummates the entire Gospel of John by showing that Christ's heavenly ministry and the apostles' ministry on the earth cooperate together to carry out God's New Testament economy.

In John 10:10, 11, and 16 the Lord unveiled to the disciples that He was the good Shepherd who came that the sheep might have life abundantly.

First, the Lord's shepherding was in His earthly ministry (Matt. 9:36). The Lord saw the Israelites as sheep harassed by their leaders; they were cast away like sheep not having a shepherd. The Lord as the Shepherd of God's elect prayed, and God told His sent One to appoint twelve apostles that they might take care of the sheep of God (10:1-6).

Second, the Lord's shepherding is in His heavenly ministry (1 Pet. 5:4) to take care of the church of God, issuing in His Body.

When the Lord stayed with His disciples after His resurrection and before His ascension, in one of His appearings, He commissioned Peter to feed His lambs and shepherd His sheep in His absence, while He is in the heavens (John 21:15-17). Shepherding implies feeding, but it includes much more than feeding. To shepherd is to take all-inclusive tender care of the flock.

This is to incorporate the apostolic ministry with Christ's heavenly ministry to take care of God's flock, which is the church that issues in the Body of Christ.

In Acts 20:28 Paul told the elders of Ephesus, "Take heed to yourselves and to all the flock, among whom the Holy Spirit has placed you as overseers to shepherd the church of God, which He obtained [or, purchased] through His own blood." Although Paul was on an urgent trip back to Jerusalem, while he was journeying, he sent word for the elders in Ephesus to come to him.

Paul said that "fierce wolves will come in among you, not sparing the flock" (v. 29). The flock is the church.

Paul says in Hebrews 13:20, "God...brought up from the dead our Lord Jesus, the great Shepherd of the sheep, in the blood of an eternal covenant." The eternal covenant is the covenant of the new testament to gain a flock, which is the church issuing in the Body and consummating the New Jerusalem. The eternal covenant of God is to consummate the New Jerusalem by the shepherding. God raised up our Lord from the dead to be the great Shepherd to consummate the New Jerusalem according to God's eternal covenant. (*CWWL, 1994-1997,* vol. 4, "Crystallization-study of the Gospel of John," pp. 446-448)

Further Reading: CWWL, 1994-1997, vol. 4, "Crystallization-study of the Gospel of John," ch. 13

Enlightenment and inspiration: _____

_____

_____

_____

Morning Nourishment

1 Pet. Therefore the elders among you I exhort, who am a
5:1-2 fellow elder and witness of the sufferings of Christ,
who am also a partaker of the glory to be revealed:
Shepherd the flock of God among you, overseeing not
under compulsion but willingly, according to God; not
by seeking gain through base means but eagerly.

Peter was so impressed with this commission of the Lord that
in his first book he tells the believers that they were like sheep
being led astray, but they have now returned to the Shepherd and
Overseer (Christ) of their souls (2:25). Christ's shepherding of His
flock includes His caring for their outward things and also their
inner being, their souls. He takes care of the things concerning
their souls by overseeing their souls. Christ indwells us to be our
life and everything, but He is also overseeing, observing, the condition and situation of our inner being. (*CWWL, 1994-1997,* vol. 4,
"Crystallization-study of the Gospel of John," p. 448)

Today's Reading

In his first Epistle, Peter speaks of Christ being the Shepherd and Overseer of our soul, our inner being and real person
(2:25). Then in 5:1-2 he tells the elders that their obligation is to
shepherd God's flock according to God. *According to God* means
that we must live God. We must have God on hand. We have God
in our understanding, in our theology, and in our teaching, but
we may not live God when we are shepherding people. When we
are one with God, we become God. Then we have God and are
God in our shepherding of others. To shepherd according to God
is to shepherd according to what God is in His attributes. God is
love, light, holiness, and righteousness. "According to God" is at
least according to these four attributes of God. We must shepherd the young ones, the weak ones, and the backsliding ones
according to these four attributes. Then we will be good shepherds. (*CWWL, 1994-1997,* vol. 5, "The Vital Groups," p. 114)

To oversee according to God means according to God's nature,
desire, way, and glory, not according to man's preference, interest,

and purpose. The elders should not oversee according to their opinion, concept, or likes or dislikes. Instead, they should oversee according to God's choice, desire, intention, and preference. The elders must oversee the church altogether according to God's thought, feeling, will, and choice. (*Life-study of 1 Peter,* p. 293)

Peter's word [in 1 Peter 5:1-4] indicates that the heavenly ministry of Christ is mainly to shepherd the church of God as His flock, which issues in His Body.

The main purpose and goal of the apostolic ministry incorporated with Christ's heavenly ministry are to build up the Body of Christ, which will consummate the New Jerusalem for the accomplishment of the eternal economy of God.

This matter of shepherding God's flock for the main purpose and ultimate consummation of the eternal economy of God is referred to even in Song of Songs. In this book Christ shepherds His seeker and pursuer.

In Song of Songs 1:7a the seeker says, "Tell me, you whom my soul loves, Where do you pasture your flock [for satisfaction]? / Where do you make it lie down at noon [for rest]?"

The Shepherd responds to the seeker by saying, "Go forth on the footsteps of the flock, / And pasture your young goats / By the shepherds' tents" (v. 8b). Under the Lord as the Chief Shepherd there are many other shepherds. The many shepherds pasture their young by their tents, that is, where they live.

Song of Songs 2:16 says, "My beloved is mine, and I am his; / He pastures his flock among the lilies [the seekers of Christ who live a life of trusting in God with a single heart]." The Lord is pasturing all His seekers as lilies, taking care of them, feeding them, and shepherding them that they may grow.

Song of Songs 6:3 says, "I am my beloved's, and my beloved is mine; / He pastures his flock among the lilies." To shepherd the believers is very crucial for their growth in life. (*CWWL, 1994-1997,* vol. 4, "Crystallization-study of the Gospel of John," pp. 448-449)

Further Reading: CWWL, 1994-1997, vol. 5, "The Vital Groups," ch. 7

Enlightenment and inspiration: _____

_____

_____

_____

Morning Nourishment

1 Pet. Nor as lording it over your allotments but by be-
5:3 coming patterns of the flock.
John I am the good Shepherd; the good Shepherd lays
10:11 down His life for the sheep.

John 21 is a chapter on shepherding....This chapter is not merely an appendix but also the completion and consummation of the Gospel of John, a book on Christ being God coming to be our life....Eventually, such a book has a conclusion on shepherding. If we do not know what shepherding is, the entire Gospel of John will be in vain to us. It is only when we shepherd others that we can know John in an intrinsic way. Shepherding is the key to the Gospel of John.

John 21:15 says, "Jesus said to Simon Peter, Simon, son of John, do you love Me more than these? He said to Him, Yes, Lord, You know that I love You." Peter said, "Lord, You know," because he had denied the Lord three times. He lost his natural confidence in his love toward the Lord. In restoring Peter's love toward Him, the Lord charged him to shepherd and feed His sheep. (*CWWL, 1994-1997,* vol. 5, "The Vital Groups," p. 114)

Today's Reading

Without John 21 the Gospel of John does not have an adequate and complete ending. [We need to take] the shepherding way to preach the gospel and revive the church. (*CWWL, 1994-1997,* vol. 4, "Crystallization-study of the Gospel of John," pp. 449-450)

First Peter 5:3 says, "Nor as lording it over your allotments but by becoming patterns of the flock." To lord it over others is to exercise lordship over those who are ruled (Matt. 20:25). Among the believers, besides Christ there should be no lord. All should be servants, even slaves (Matt. 20:26-27; 23:10-11). The elders in the church can only take the leadership (not the lordship), which all the believers should honor and follow (1 Thes. 5:12; 1 Tim. 5:17).

All the elders should be slaves of the saints. It is not adequate for the elders even to be servants; they must be slaves. This is something Peter learned from the Lord Himself. Peter heard the Lord Jesus say that those who desire to become great must be slaves. Elders should regard themselves as slaves, and the brothers and sisters as their masters.

Literally, the word *allotments* means "lots, portions"; hence, "allotments, portions entrusted." Here this word refers to the flock. The churches are God's possession, allotted to the elders as their allotments, their portions, entrusted to them by God for their care.

The church is God's flock and His possession. The elders have been appointed by God to be shepherds of the flock. Hence, God has allotted the church in their locality to them for their care. The church in a particular locality is God's possession; it is not the possession of the elders. But God has allotted that church to the elders so that they may care for it and shepherd it. Furthermore, the church is only allotted to the elders for their care temporarily. For eternity the church is God's possession. Even the elders themselves are a part of the church as the possession of God.

Instead of lording it over the allotments, the elders should become patterns of the flock. This means that they take the lead to serve and care for the church so that the believers may follow. (*Life-study of 1 Peter,* pp. 294-295)

Shepherding and teaching are our obligation as a charge given to us by the Lord. This is the basic way ordained by God in the building up of the Body of Christ to consummate His eternal goal—the New Jerusalem....The Gospels reveal Christ's shepherding and teaching in His ministry for carrying out God's eternal economy. (*CWWL, 1994-1997,* vol. 5, "The Vital Groups," p. 105)

I care for only one thing—to carry out what the Lord has charged us to do. We all need to rise up and put everything of the unscriptural practice of Christianity under our feet. The number one thing we should do in these days is to visit people in their homes. This is to follow the pattern of the Lord Jesus. We must go to visit people. (*CWWL, 1986,* vol. 3, "Elders' Training, Book 9: The Eldership and the God-ordained Way (1)," pp. 38-39)

Further Reading: CWWL, 1994-1997, vol. 5, "The Vital Groups," ch. 6

Enlightenment and inspiration: _____

_____

_____

_____

Morning Nourishment

Matt. And seeing the crowds, He was moved with com-
9:36 passion for them, because they were harassed and
      cast away like sheep not having a shepherd.
Luke And he rose up and came to his own father. But
15:20 while he was still a long way off, his father saw him
      and was moved with compassion, and he ran and
      fell on his neck and kissed him affectionately.

Luke 15:4 says, "Which man of you, who has a hundred
sheep and has lost one of them, does not leave the ninety-nine
in the wilderness and go after the one which is lost until he
finds it?" Here the "wilderness" signifies the world. The shepherd going into the wilderness to seek the lost sheep indicates
that the Son has come to the world to be with men (John 1:14).

Luke 15:5-6 continues, "And when he finds it, he lays it on his
shoulders, rejoicing. And when he comes into his house, he calls
together his friends and his neighbors, saying to them, Rejoice
with me, for I have found my sheep that was lost." Here we see
the Savior's saving strength and His saving love. (*Life-study of
Luke*, p. 291)

Today's Reading

Shepherding is something divine. In order to be a shepherd, we
must be a witness of Christ, a member of Christ, and a brother of
Christ, sharing His sonship....We need to shepherd people. This is
the way to be fruitful, to have the multiplication and the increase. If
this kind of fellowship is received by us, I believe there will be a big
revival on the earth, not by a few spiritual giants but by the many
members of Christ's Body being shepherds who follow the steps of
the processed Triune God in seeking and gaining fallen people.
(*CWWL, 1994-1997*, vol. 5, "The Vital Groups," pp. 92-93)

The spirit of not shepherding and seeking others and being
without love and forgiveness is spreading in the recovery every-
where. I believe that not having the Father's loving and forgiving heart and not having the Savior's shepherding and seeking
spirit is the reason for our barrenness. I realize that you all

work hard, but there is almost no fruit. (*CWWL, 1994-1997,* vol. 5, "A Word of Love to the Co-workers, Elders, Lovers, and Seekers of the Lord," p. 31)

To cherish people is to make them happy, pleasant, and comfortable; to nourish people is to feed them with the all-inclusive Christ in His full ministry in His three stages....He takes care of the churches as the lampstands in His humanity as the Son of Man to cherish them.

He is also the High Priest with His divinity as the "energy belt" to nourish us with Himself....His nourishing the churches in His divinity is so that the churches may grow and mature in His divine life and become the overcomers in His sevenfold intensification. (*CWWL, 1994-1997,* vol. 5, "The Vital Groups," pp. 151, 158)

While the Lord Jesus was enjoying a feast with tax collectors and sinners, the Pharisees criticized and condemned Him, and they asked the disciples why their teacher ate with such people (Matt. 9:10-11). The Lord took the opportunity...to give a very pleasant revelation of Himself as the Physician: "Those who are strong have no need of a physician, but those who are ill" (v. 12). The Lord was telling the Pharisees that the tax collectors and sinners were "patients," sick ones, and that to them He was not a judge but a physician, a healer....The judgment of a judge is according to righteousness, whereas the healing of a physician is according to mercy and grace. Those whom the Lord made people of His heavenly kingdom were lepers (Matt. 8:2-4), paralytics (8:5-13; 9:2-8), the fever-ridden (8:14-15), the demon-possessed (8:16, 28-32), those sick of all kinds of illnesses (8:16), the despised tax collectors, and sinners (9:9-11)....He came to minister as a physician, to heal, recover, enliven, and save them so that they might be reconstituted to be citizens of the kingdom of the heavens. (*The Conclusion of the New Testament,* pp. 490-491)

Further Reading: CWWL, 1994-1997, vol. 5, "The Vital Groups," chs. 4, 11; "A Word of Love to the Co-workers, Elders, Lovers, and Seekers of the Lord," ch. 2

Enlightenment and inspiration: _____

_____

_____

_____

Morning Nourishment

Heb. Now the God of peace, He who brought up from the
13:20 dead our Lord Jesus, the great Shepherd of the
sheep, in the blood of an eternal covenant.
Rev. And in the midst of the lampstands One like the Son
1:13 of Man, clothed with a garment reaching to the feet,
and girded about at the breasts with a golden girdle.

When Christ as the God-Savior wanted to save an immoral
woman of Samaria, He traveled from Judea to Galilee through Samaria, He detoured from the main way of Samaria to the city of
Sychar, and He waited at the well of Jacob, near Sychar, for His ob-
ject to come that He might cherish her by asking her to give Him
something to drink so that He might nourish her with the water of
life, which is the flowing Triune God Himself (John 4:1-14)....He
waited at the well of Jacob for her to come in order to cherish her so
that she could be nourished with the living water of the Triune
God. (*CWWL, 1994-1997,* vol. 5, "The Vital Groups," p. 149)

Today's Reading

[In John 8 a] sinful woman was accused by the scribes and
Pharisees, but eventually they were condemned by Christ. None
of them could condemn her, and they all left. The Lord said to the
woman, "Has no one condemned you?" She said, "No one, Lord."
Then He said, "Neither do I condemn you" (vv. 10-11). This is cherishing. None of the scribes and Pharisees could say that he was
without sin. The Son of Man is the unique One without sin, so He
was the only one qualified to condemn the sinful woman, but He
would not do it. He came not to condemn the lost but to save them.

The first gospel preacher, Christ, carried out His ministry by
shepherding. He went to Jericho just to visit one person, a chief tax
collector (Luke 19:1-10). He did not go there to hold a big gospel
campaign with thousands of people. His desire was to preach the
gospel to gain one person, and His preaching was a shepherding.

When His disciples rejected people bringing their children to
Him, He stopped their preventing and asked them to bring the
children to Him, and He cherished the parents by laying His hands

on their children (Matt. 19:13-15). The disciples' preventing surely offended the parents. Quite often we are preventing people instead of cherishing people. The Lord stopped the disciples' preventing.

While Christ was being crucified on the cross, two robbers were crucified with Him (27:38). One of them said, "Jesus, remember me when You come into Your kingdom" (Luke 23:42). Jesus said to him, "Truly I say to you, Today you shall be with Me in Paradise" (v. 43). The first one saved by Christ through His crucifixion was not a gentleman but a criminal, a robber, sentenced to death. This is very meaningful.

Christ is the best model of cherishing and nourishing as seen in Revelation 1. In verses 12 and 13 John said, "I turned to see the voice that spoke with me; and when I turned, I saw seven golden lampstands, and in the midst of the lampstands One like the Son of Man, clothed with a garment reaching to the feet, and girded about at the breasts with a golden girdle." This shows that Christ is taking care of the lampstands by being the Son of Man with a long garment. This garment is the priestly robe (Exo. 28:33-35), which shows that Christ is our great High Priest. (*CWWL, 1994-1997*, vol. 5, "The Vital Groups," pp. 135-136, 113, 148, 123, 154)

In 2 Thessalonians 3:7-9 Paul reminds the Thessalonians that, in the matter of orderly living, the apostles were a pattern to them: "For you yourselves know how you ought to imitate us, because we were not disorderly among you; nor did we eat bread as a gift from anyone, but in labor and hardship we worked night and day so that we would not be burdensome to any of you; not because we do not have the right, but in order that we might give ourselves to you as a pattern that you might imitate us." The apostles were for the building up of the church in all things (2 Cor. 12:19). They were absolutely not disorderly among the believers but were a pattern for the believers to imitate. (*Life-study of 2 Thessalonians*, p. 57)

Further Reading: CWWL, 1994-1997, vol. 5, "The Vital Groups," chs. 9-10

Enlightenment and inspiration: _____

_____

_____

_____

Morning Nourishment

1 Thes. But we were gentle in your midst, as a nursing
2:7 mother would cherish her own children.
11 Just as you know how *we were* to each one of you,
as a father to his own children, exhorting you and
consoling *you* and testifying.

Although the word *fostering* cannot be found in 1 Thessalonians 2, the fact of fostering can be seen in this chapter. Here Paul likens the apostles both to a nursing mother and to an exhorting father. This means that the apostles were mothers and fathers to the new believers. They regarded the believers as children under their fostering care. Just as parents care for their children, fostering their growth, so the apostles cared for the new believers. Thus, in 1 Thessalonians 2 we see the fostering of a holy life for the church life. In verses 1 through 12 we have the care of a nursing mother and an exhorting father, and in verses 13 through 20 we see the reward given to those who foster believers in this way. Because the apostles rendered such a care to the new believers, the apostles will eventually receive a reward from the Lord.

First Thessalonians 2:1-12 surely is a word to new believers. In these verses we do not have much that is weighty or deep. Here we do not have profound doctrines. Instead, we have a word that can be compared to the way parents speak to young children. Let us consider this portion verse by verse so that we may be impressed how to help new believers. (*Life-study of 1 Thessalonians*, pp. 96-97)

Today's Reading

In Acts 20 Paul told the elders of the church in Ephesus, "You yourselves know, from the first day that I set foot in Asia, how I was with you all the time" (v. 18). Paul was with the saints in Ephesus for three years. He not only taught them publicly in meetings but also taught them from house to house (v. 20). Night and day, he did not cease admonishing each one of the saints with tears (v. 31). This teaches us how to perfect the saints.

(*CWWL, 1986,* vol. 3, "Elders' Training Book 9: The Eldership and the God-ordained Way (1)," p. 115)

In 1 Corinthians Paul was like a father disciplining his children. But even this discipline came out of a deep, intimate concern. For example, a mother may spank one of her children. But while he is receiving that spanking, the child realizes that the mother is disciplining him with a loving spirit and attitude. Thus, even when she is spanking her child, she can love him. Children can tell whether or not their parents discipline them out of a spirit of love. It was with a loving, concerned spirit that Paul wrote the book of 1 Corinthians. To be sure, in 2 Corinthians as a whole, and especially in chapter 7, we see Paul's intimate concern for the believers.

[In 2 Corinthians 12:15 Paul says], "I will most gladly spend and be utterly spent on behalf of your souls. If I love you more abundantly, am I loved less?" In this verse "spend" means to spend what he has, referring to his possessions. To "be utterly spent" means to spend what he is, referring to his being. Paul was willing to sacrifice himself—his soul, his life, his entire being—for the believers. He was also willing to give all his money and material possessions. The Lord Jesus gave His soul for us; He was utterly spent for us. In like manner, Paul's desire was to be utterly spent for the Corinthians. All the saints in the Lord's recovery need to learn this crucial lesson: to receive grace to spend what we have and to be utterly spent for the saints and for the churches. (*Life-study of 2 Corinthians,* pp. 383, 498-499)

I hope that there will be a genuine revival among us by our receiving this burden of shepherding. If all the churches receive this teaching to participate in Christ's wonderful shepherding, there will be a big revival in the recovery. (*CWWL, 1994-1997,* vol. 5, "The Vital Groups," p. 92)

Further Reading: Watchman Nee—a Seer of the Divine Revelation in the Present Age, ch. 11

Enlightenment and inspiration: _____

_____

_____

_____

Hymns, #1221

1   Jesus, our wonderful Shepherd
     Brought us right out of the fold
  Into His pasture so plenteous,
     Into His riches untold.

     Glorious church life,
     Feasting from such a rich store!
     Here where we're dwelling in oneness
     God commands life evermore.

2   In the divisions He sought us,
     Weary and famished for food;
  Into the good land He brought us,
     Oh, to our spirit how good!

3   Jesus Himself is our pasture,
     He is the food that we eat;
  We as His sheep are fed richly
     Each time, whenever we meet.

4   Dwell we here on a high mountain,
     Wet with the morning-fresh dew,
  Slaking our thirst at the fountain,
     Water so living and new.

5   Christ is our rest and enjoyment,
     Here we have nothing to fear;
  Here all the sheep dwell securely,
     Kept by His presence so dear.

Composition for prophecy with main point and sub-points: _____

Being Fully Reconciled to God
and Enlarged in Heart
to Represent God Rightly in His Economy

Scripture Reading: 2 Cor. 5:18-20; 6:11-13; 10:8; 12:15; 13:4, 10

Day 1   I. **In order to represent God in His economy, we need to be fully reconciled to God (2 Cor. 5:20):**
   A. The ministry of reconciliation is to bring us back to God fully, thoroughly, completely, and entirely (v. 18):
      1. The ministry of reconciliation is not merely to bring sinners back to God but, even the more, to bring believers absolutely into God (vv. 19-20).
      2. Until we are wholly one with the Lord, being in Him and allowing Him to be in us absolutely, we will need the ministry of reconciliation.

Day 2   B. Two steps are required for us to be fully reconciled to God (vv. 19-20):
      1. In 2 Corinthians 5:19 it is the world that is reconciled to God, but in verse 20 it is the believers, who have already been reconciled to God and are to be reconciled further to God.
      2. The first step of reconciliation is to reconcile sinners to God from sin (v. 19):
         a. For this purpose Christ died for our sins that they might be forgiven by God (1 Cor. 15:3; Luke 24:46-47; 1 John 2:12).
         b. This is the objective aspect of Christ's death; in this aspect He bore our sins upon Himself on the cross that they might be judged by God for us (1 Pet. 2:24; Isa. 53:11-12; Heb. 9:28; Col. 1:22; Rom. 8:3).
      3. The second step of reconciliation is to reconcile believers living in the natural life to God from the flesh (2 Cor. 5:20):

      a. For this purpose Christ died for us—the persons—that we might live to Him in the resurrection life (vv. 14-15).

      b. Because we are still separated from God and because we are not fully one with God and altogether in harmony with Him, we need the second step of reconciliation.

      c. The subjective aspect of the death of Christ needs to be applied to our situation and to our natural life (Rom. 6:6; 8:13; Gal. 5:24; Matt. 16:24):

        (1) In order that we may be reconciled to God in full, the Father exposes our natural life and unveils our real situation to us (1 John 1:5, 7):

          (a) As a result, we condemn our natural being and apply the cross subjectively, and this application of the death of Christ crucifies our natural life.

          (b) As our natural man is crossed out, we experience the second step of reconciliation; in this step the veil of our natural man is rent so that we may live in God's presence.

        (2) Instead of taking place once for all, the second step of reconciliation is continuous.

    4. By the two aspects of His death, Christ fully reconciles God's chosen people to God (Rom. 5:10; 2 Cor. 5:19-20).

Day 3   **II. Being fully reconciled to God causes us to be enlarged in our heart (v. 20; 6:11-13):**

    A. How large our heart is depends on the degree of our reconciliation to God.

    B. Narrowness of heart is a strong indication that

we have been reconciled to God only partially
and that the percentage of our salvation is quite
low (v. 12; Rom. 5:10).

C. In order to be strict with ourselves and not with
others, we need to be enlarged; those who are
constricted are usually narrow as well, and thus
they need to have their heart enlarged (2 Cor.
6:12-13).

D. Wisdom and largeness of heart are two aspects
of one thing; the secret of wisdom is to have a
large heart (1 Kings 4:20, 29).

Day 4 **III. When we have been fully reconciled to God
and have been enlarged in heart, we can represent God rightly in His economy (2 Cor.
5:20; 10:8; 12:15; 13:4, 10):**

A. Because the apostle Paul had been fully reconciled to God and enlarged in heart, he was qualified to be an ambassador of Christ, representing
God (5:20):

1. An ambassador of Christ is one who represents God, the highest authority in the universe:

a. God has given all authority in heaven
and on earth to Christ (Matt. 28:18).

b. Jesus is the Christ—the Lord of all, the
King of kings and the Lord of lords—the
highest authority (Acts 2:36; 10:36; 1 Tim.
6:15; Rev. 17:14; 19:16).

c. The Lord needs some ambassadors on
earth who are qualified to represent Him
(Matt. 28:19).

d. A new covenant minister is one who has
been authorized with the heavenly authority to represent the highest authority (2 Cor. 3:6; 5:20):

(1) The apostles were commissioned to
represent Christ to accomplish God's
purpose (Matt. 10:40; John 13:20;
Gal. 4:14b).

Day 5

          (2) All the members of the Body are representatives of the Head, His ambassadors (Acts 9:6, 10-17; 22:12-16).

    2. As an ambassador of Christ, Paul was "the acting God" (2 Cor. 1:3-4, 12, 15-16; 2:10; 10:1; 11:2):

      a. Paul was one with Christ to be the acting God in comforting the believers (1:3-4).

      b. Paul conducted himself in the singleness of God, for he was an imitator of the simple God, and he lived God (v. 12).

      c. Paul's coming to the Corinthians was the coming of God as grace (vv. 15-16).

      d. Paul forgave a particular matter in the person of Christ (2:10).

      e. Paul entreated the believers through the meekness and gentleness of Christ (10:1).

      f. Paul was jealous over the saints with the jealousy of God (11:2).

B. We need to learn a serious lesson from the one time that Moses failed to represent God (Num. 20:2-13):

    1. In striking the rock twice and in calling the people rebels, Moses did not sanctify God in the sight of the people of Israel (vv. 10-12):

      a. To sanctify God is to make Him holy, that is, separate from the false gods; to fail to sanctify God is to make Him common (v. 12).

      b. In being angry with the people and in wrongly striking the rock twice, Moses failed to sanctify God (vv. 10-11).

      c. In being angry when God was not angry, Moses failed to represent God rightly in His holy nature, and in striking the rock twice, he did not keep God's word in His economy (vv. 10-12).

      d. Moses offended both God's holy nature and His divine economy; he condemned

the people as rebels, but he was the one
who rebelled against God's word (vv. 10,
24; 27:14).

2. In all that we say and do concerning God's
people, our attitude must be according to
God's holy nature, and our actions must be
according to His divine economy.

3. If we do not sanctify God in our attitude and
actions, we rebel against Him and offend Him.

Day 6   C. A person who represents God rightly must have
the following qualifications:

1. He must submit to authority (Matt. 8:8-9).

2. He must realize that in himself he has no
authority (28:18; 2 Cor. 10:8; 13:10).

3. He must know God and God's will (Eph. 1:9;
5:17).

4. He must be one who denies the self (Matt.
16:24).

5. He must be one with the Lord and live in
constant and intimate fellowship with Him
(1 Cor. 6:17; 1:9; 1 John 1:3).

6. He must not be subjective and not act according to his own feeling (2 Cor. 3:5).

7. He must be kind and gracious in dealing
with others (Luke 6:35; cf. Rom. 5:15-16; 1 Cor.
2:12).

8. He must be a person in resurrection, living
in the resurrection life of Christ (2 Cor. 1:9;
4:14; Num. 17:1-10).

9. He must take a lowly place before God (14:5;
16:3-4, 22, 45; Matt. 11:29; Rom. 12:16; Luke
14:7-11; 1 Pet. 5:5-6).

10. He must be able to bear offenses (Exo. 16:7;
Num. 14:2, 5, 9, 27; Matt. 6:14-15; 1 Cor. 4:6-13).

11. He must have a consciousness of his inability and unsuitability (Exo. 3:11; 4:6-7, 10;
2 Cor. 3:5; 1 Cor. 15:10).

12. He must be one who represents God properly
(Exo. 32:11-12; 2 Cor. 5:18, 20; Eph. 6:20).

Morning Nourishment

2 Cor. But all things are out from God, who has reconciled
5:18-20 us to Himself through Christ and has given to us the
ministry of reconciliation; namely, that God in Christ
was reconciling the world to Himself, not accounting
their offenses to them, and has put in us the word of
reconciliation. On behalf of Christ then we are ambassadors, as God entreats *you* through us; we beseech *you* on behalf of Christ, Be reconciled to God.

It is imperative that an authority represent God properly.
Whether in wrath or in compassion, he should be like God all
the time. If we are wrong, we should confess that we are wrong;
we should never drag God into our mistake. If we do, we will
bring judgment upon ourselves....It is a serious thing to drag
God into our mistakes. (*CWWN,* vol. 47, "Authority and Submission," p. 254)

Before we were saved, we were enemies of God, and there
was no peace between us and God. Instead of peace, we were at
enmity with God. But when we repented and believed in the
Lord Jesus, His blood washed away our sins, and we received
God's forgiveness. As a result, we were justified by God and reconciled to Him. Having been reconciled to God in this way, there
was no longer enmity between us and God....[However], this
understanding of reconciliation...is not the full significance of
reconciliation as ministered by the apostle Paul.

The ministry of reconciliation is not merely to bring sinners
back to God, but, even the more, to bring believers absolutely into
God. Hence, it is not sufficient simply to be brought back to God;
we must also be in Him. (*Life-study of 2 Corinthians,* p. 342)

Today's Reading

As genuine believers, we can testify that we are in Him. But
are we in Christ in a practical way in our daily living? For example,...when you make a joke, do you have the assurance that you
are in Him?...There is no neutral ground: we are either in Christ
or outside of Him. Because we are not always in Christ in a

practical way, we need further reconciliation. We need to be reconciled back into Christ.

The biblical understanding of reconciliation includes more than merely being brought back to God. It is to be brought back into Him. Therefore, according to the Bible, to bring others to God means to bring them into God and to make them absolutely one with Him,...mingled with Him....Biblical oneness with God is a oneness in which we enter into God and God enters into us. Therefore, the Lord Jesus said, "Abide in Me and I in you" (John 15:4). He did not say, "Abide *with* Me and I *with* you."

Until we are wholly one with the Lord, being in Him and allowing Him to be in us absolutely, we shall continue to need the ministry of reconciliation, the ministry with which Paul was commissioned. Paul was commissioned with the work of bringing the believers into God in a way that was absolute and practical. Once we see this, we are qualified to understand the last part of 2 Corinthians 5 and the first part of chapter 6....The conjunction "and" at the beginning of 6:1 indicates that chapter 6 is a continuation of the last part of chapter 5.

I urge you not to cling to your old, limited concept of reconciliation....I would encourage you to take in this new, fuller understanding of reconciliation and see that to be reconciled is to be brought into God and that the ministry of reconciliation is the ministry of bringing others into God.

There were many problems among the believers at Corinth. All those problems were signs that those believers were not absolutely in God. In many particular matters they were not in God. Although they had been saved and born of God, they were not living in Him. For this reason, concerning many items in their daily living, they were outside of God. Therefore, Paul was burdened to bring them into God. This is to reconcile them to God. (*Life-study of 2 Corinthians,* pp. 343-345)

Further Reading: Life-study of 2 Corinthians, msgs. 37, 39; *Life-study of Exodus,* msgs. 100-102

Enlightenment and inspiration: _____

_____

_____

_____

Morning Nourishment

2 Cor. For the love of Christ constrains us because we
5:14-15 have judged this, that One died for all, therefore all
died; and He died for all that those who live may no
longer live to themselves but to Him who died for
them and has been raised.

In 2 Corinthians 5:20...Paul's use of the word *ambassadors* indicates that the apostles are commissioned with a definite ministry; they represent Christ to accomplish God's purpose.

In verse 19 it is the world that is reconciled to God; in verse 20 it is the believers, who have already been reconciled to God, who need to be reconciled to God further. This clearly indicates that there are two steps for men to be fully reconciled to God. The first step is as sinners to be reconciled to God from sin. For this purpose Christ died for our sins (1 Cor. 15:3) that they may be forgiven by God. This is the objective aspect of Christ's death. In this aspect He bore our sins on the cross that they might be judged by God upon Him for us. The second step is as believers living in the natural life to be reconciled to God from the flesh. For this purpose Christ died for us—the persons—that we may live to Him in the resurrection life (2 Cor. 5:14-15). This is the subjective aspect of Christ's death. In this aspect, He was made sin for us so that we might be judged and done away with by God in order that we may become the righteousness of God in Him. By the two aspects of His death, He has fully reconciled God's chosen people to God. (*Life-study of 2 Corinthians,* p. 126)

Today's Reading

These two steps of reconciliation are clearly portrayed by the two veils of the tabernacle. The first veil is called the screen (Exo. 26:37). A sinner was brought to God through the reconciliation of the atoning blood to enter into the Holy Place by passing this screen. This typifies the first step of reconciliation. The second veil (Exo. 26:31-35; Heb. 9:3) still separated him from God who is in the Holy of Holies. This veil needed to be rent that he might be brought to God in the Holy of Holies. This is the second step of reconciliation. The Corinthian believers had been reconciled to God, having passed through the first veil and having entered into the Holy Place. Yet, they still lived in the flesh. They needed to pass the second veil, which has been rent already (Matt. 27:51; Heb. 10:20) to enter into the Holy of Holies to live with God in their spirit (1 Cor. 6:17). The goal of this Epistle is to bring them here that they may be persons in the spirit (1 Cor. 2:14), in the Holy of Holies. (*Life-study of 2 Corinthians,* pp. 126-127)

The second step of reconciliation is much deeper than the first step, for it takes place not in the outer court outside the tabernacle but within the Holy Place inside the tabernacle. Instead of taking place once for all, this kind of reconciliation is continuous. If you consider your experience, you will realize that no matter how long you have been a seeking Christian, you still have the sense deep within that you are separated from God's presence by something, mainly by your natural life, your old man, your self. You may be very good, nice, pious, "holy," and "spiritual," yet you know that there is still something separating you from God's presence. You are not fully one with God, altogether in harmony with Him. Instead, because you are still separated from Him, you need the second step of reconciliation. You need the application of the subjective death of Christ to…your natural life.…This application…crucifies your natural life, rending the veil that separates you from God's inner presence.

In order that we may be reconciled to God in full, the Father exposes our natural life and unveils our real situation to us. As a result, we condemn our natural being and apply the cross subjectively. Then as our natural man is crossed out, we experience the second step of reconciliation. In this step the veil of our natural man is rent so that we may live in God's presence. (*The Conclusion of the New Testament,* pp. 1586-1587)

Further Reading: *Life-study of 2 Corinthians,* msgs. 14, 46; *The Conclusion of the New Testament,* msg. 146; *CWWL, 1994-1997,* vol. 3, "Crystallization-study of Song of Songs," chs. 10-12

Enlightenment and inspiration: _____

_____

_____

_____

Morning Nourishment

2 Cor. **Our mouth is opened to you, Corinthians; our**
6:11-13 **heart is enlarged. You are not constricted in us, but**
you are constricted in your inward parts. But for a
recompense in kind, I speak as to children, you
also be enlarged.

If we would be fully reconciled to God, fully saved, we need to be enlarged in our heart. [In 2 Corinthians 6:12-13] Paul appealed to the Corinthians to be enlarged....To be enlarged requires the aspects of the all-fitting life covered in verses 3 through 10. It requires the eighteen items beginning with "in": in endurance, in afflictions, in necessities, in distresses, in stripes, in imprisonments, in tumults, in labors, in watchings, in fastings, in pureness, in knowledge, in long-suffering, in kindness, in a holy spirit, in unfeigned love, in the word of truth, in the power of God. It also requires the three pairs starting with "through": through the weapons of righteousness on the right hand and on the left, through glory and dishonor, through evil report and good report. Finally, it requires all the seven pairs beginning with "as": as deceivers and yet true, as unknown and yet well known, as dying and yet behold we live, as being disciplined and yet not being put to death, as made sorrowful yet always rejoicing, as poor yet enriching many, as having nothing and yet possessing all things. If we have all these characteristics of the all-fitting life, all the items with "in," "through," and "as," we have truly been enlarged. (*Life-study of 2 Corinthians*, pp. 367-368)

Today's Reading

In the past fifty years I have known many dear and precious brothers who were elders and co-workers. A good number of these brothers were very strict and straight. Regarding the Lord's word in Matthew 10:16 to be "prudent as serpents," these straight ones could not at all be "as serpents." Neither could they be "as deceivers and yet true" [2 Cor. 6:8]. To be true here means to be straight. The brothers to whom I am referring were not only strict; they were extremely straight. For example, one such brother might say, "Oh, that person shouldn't be in the church. Cast him out!

How can we possibly accept him? Oh, that sister is awful. She should be condemned." Many times we tried our best to convince these straight brothers to be more flexible. We might say, "This one is a real brother in the Lord. No doubt, he is wrong in certain things. But we still must embrace him by forgiving him and by giving him an opportunity to improve." Nevertheless, sometimes a straight brother would respond by saying, "No! That is not the biblical way!" This attitude is a clear indication that those who are strict and straight in this way need to be enlarged.

We need to be straight and strict. However, we should be strict with ourselves, not with others. In order to be strict with ourselves and not with others, we need to be enlarged. Those who are very straight are usually narrow as well. They need to have their hearts enlarged.

When we become enlarged in our heart, we should not become loose. Rather, we should continue to be strict and straight concerning ourselves, but we should not apply this principle to others. If the Lord has done such a work in us, we have been enlarged.

I would ask you to consider once again all the matters covered by Paul in 2 Corinthians 6:3-10. If we have all these characteristics and qualifications, we shall have a large heart. We may be outwardly very small, but our heart will be like an ocean. But if we do not have these qualifications, we shall have a very small heart. We may be great in our own eyes, yet our heart may be extremely narrow. For example, our attitude may be that if a certain one makes a mistake, we should have nothing to do with him unless he repents. This is a sign of narrowness. It is also an indication that we are not able to reconcile others to God, for we ourselves have not been fully reconciled to Him. Our narrowness is a strong indication that we have been reconciled to God only partially and that the percentage of our salvation is quite low. How large our heart is depends on the degree of our reconciliation to God. (*Life-study of 2 Corinthians,* pp. 368-369)

Further Reading: Life-study of 2 Corinthians, msgs. 41-42

Enlightenment and inspiration: _____

_____

_____

_____

Morning Nourishment

Eph. For which I am an ambassador in a chain, that in it
6:20 I would speak boldly, as I ought to speak.

Matt. And Jesus came and spoke to them, saying, All
28:18-19 authority has been given to Me in heaven and on earth. Go therefore and disciple all the nations, baptizing them into the name of the Father and of the Son and of the Holy Spirit.

Paul and the other ministers of the new covenant, those who had been constituted of the processed Triune God and who were mature in life, were no doubt in the Holy of Holies. They lived in the spirit, and they were ripe, ready to be raptured. Their only goal was to please the Lord by living to Him. Spontaneously, being such persons, they were able to bring others thoroughly back to God.... These ministers of the new covenant were qualified to bring back to God anyone who had not been fully reconciled to Him.

As long as we have not been brought back to God fully, we need someone like the apostles to bring us back to Him. It does not matter whether the distance between us and God is great or small. We need to be reconciled to God entirely. The ministry of the new covenant is to bring people back to God in a full and thorough way; it is to reconcile us to God entirely and completely. (*Life-study of 2 Corinthians,* p. 123)

Today's Reading

In both 2 Corinthians 5:20 and Ephesians 6:20 Paul says that he and his co-workers were ambassadors of Christ. An ambassador is one sent by a particular authority to contact certain people. The faithful believers are ambassadors sent by God, the highest authority in the universe. They are one with God, representing God to carry out His purpose in Christ on this earth. (*The Conclusion of the New Testament,* pp. 1202-1203)

The apostle Paul was an ambassador of Christ. An ambassador is one who represents the highest authority. The United States government has many ambassadors sent out to many different countries. These ambassadors represent the government of the

United States. The highest authority in this universe is God, and God has given all authority in heaven and on earth to Christ (Matt. 28:18). God has appointed Christ to be the King of kings and the Lord of lords (1 Tim. 6:15; Rev. 17:14). Today Jesus is the Christ, the Lord of all, the highest authority. For this highest authority there is the need of some ambassadors on this earth who are qualified to represent Him. The Lord's ministry is not a matter of merely being a preacher or a teacher but of being one who is authorized with the heavenly authority, representing the highest authority in the whole universe. First, we need to be captured by Christ, and eventually, we need to become a representative of Christ on this earth to deal with the earthly nations as an ambassador.

Some Christians have the title "Ambassador of Christ" printed on their witnessing card along with their name. Many years ago I had a card that said "Bondslave of Christ—Witness Lee." At that time I did not dare to entitle myself an ambassador of Christ, but now I have a fuller realization that we all have to be ambassadors of Christ on this earth. We are not only the captives of Christ. Eventually, we have to be the ambassadors of Christ representing Him on this earth for His interests. We may think that this is something too great, too big. Maybe some of the sisters would think that they are just the weak vessels. They may wonder how they could be the ambassadors of Christ, representing the highest authority on this earth. Regardless of whether we are a brother or a sister, all of us are members of the Body of Christ. The highest authority is Christ as the Head, and we as members of the Body have to be representatives of the Head. As representatives of the Head, we are ambassadors. We should not consider that we are little or that we are too weak. Being ambassadors is not a matter of whether we are little or weak. Actually, we have to be more weak, even weak in Christ (2 Cor. 13:4). (*CWWL, 1967*, vol. 2, "An Autobiography of a Person in the Spirit," pp. 171-172)

Further Reading: The Conclusion of the New Testament, msg. 111;
  An Autobiography of a Person in the Spirit, ch. 6

Enlightenment and inspiration: _____

_____

_____

Morning Nourishment

2 Cor. For our boasting is this, the testimony of our con-
1:12 science, that in singleness and sincerity of God,...
      in the grace of God, we have conducted ourselves
      in the world, and more abundantly toward you.
2:10 But whom you forgive anything, I also *forgive;* for
      also what I have forgiven, if I have forgiven any-
      thing, *it is* for your sake in the person of Christ.

[In 2 Corinthians 2:10, *person* literally means] "face" as in 4:6, [referring to] the part around the eyes; the look as the index of the inward thoughts and feelings, which shows forth and manifests the whole person. This indicates that the apostle was one who lived and acted in the presence of Christ, according to the index of His whole person, expressed in His eyes....[Paul] wrote this Epistle [of 2 Corinthians] to comfort and encourage the saints in a very personal, tender, and affectionate way, in such a way that this Epistle can be considered to some extent his autobiography. In it we see a person who lived Christ according to what he wrote concerning Him in his first Epistle, in the closest and most intimate contact with Him, acting according to the index of His eyes; a person who was one with Christ, full of Christ, and saturated with Christ; a person who was broken and even terminated in his natural life, softened and flexible in his will, affectionate yet restricted in his emotion, considerate and sober in his mind, and pure and genuine in his spirit toward the believers for their benefit, that they might experience and enjoy Christ as he did for the fulfillment of God's eternal purpose in the building up of Christ's Body. (2 Cor. 2:10, footnote 3)

Today's Reading

The apostles' situation of death forced them to be simple, that is, not to base their confidence on themselves or on their natural human ability to work out a solution to their difficult situation. This was the testimony of their conscience and was their confidence (2 Cor. 1:15). (2 Cor. 1:12, footnote 2)

The Bible tells us that Moses was "very meek, more than

anyone else who was on the face of the earth" (Num. 12:3). A real man of God, Moses fell on his face before God, not saying anything. He had truly learned of God. Nevertheless, such a meek person became angry at the children of Israel. God had told him to take the rod and speak to the rock that it may yield its water. Moses could have gathered the congregation together before the rock and said, "Praise the Lord! He is good and He is gracious. He surely takes care of us. You need water, and He will supply water. We only need to speak to the rock, and the water will flow forth." How wonderful it would have been if Moses had spoken in this way! However, in his anger Moses said to the people, "You rebels" [Num. 20:10]....Then he struck the rock twice with his rod [v. 11]. It was not necessary for him to strike the rock once, much less twice. The rock had already been struck in Exodus 17, and God did not tell Moses to strike it again. Rather, God told Moses simply to speak to the rock. Although Moses was a faithful servant of God, in Numbers 20 he made a mistake which caused him to lose his right to enter into the promised good land. (*Life-study of Numbers*, p. 211)

To sanctify God is to make Him holy, that is, separate from all the false gods; to fail to sanctify God is to make Him common. In being angry with the people (Num. 20:10) and in wrongly striking the rock twice (v. 11), Moses failed to sanctify God. In being angry when God was not angry, Moses did not represent God rightly in His holy nature, and in striking the rock twice, he did not keep God's word in His economy....Thus, Moses offended both God's holy nature and His divine economy.

In all that we say and do concerning God's people, our attitude must be according to God's holy nature, and our actions must be according to His divine economy. This is to sanctify Him. Otherwise, in our words and deeds we will rebel against Him and offend Him. (Num. 20:12, footnote 1)

Further Reading: Life-study of Numbers, msg. 29; *CWWN,* vol. 47, "Authority and Submission," chs. 13-16

Enlightenment and inspiration: _____

_____

_____

_____

Morning Nourishment

Matt. But the centurion answered and said, Lord, I am
8:8-9 not fit for You to enter under my roof; but only
speak a word, and my servant will be healed. For I
also am a man under authority, having soldiers
under me. And I say to this one, Go, and he goes;
and to another, Come, and he comes; and to my
slave, Do this, and he does *it.*

God's children must learn to know authority and find out to
whom they should submit....As soon as we move to a place, we
should not expect to be the master, asking others to submit to us.
Instead, we should be like the centurion, who told the Lord Jesus,
"For I also am a man under authority, having soldiers under me"
(Matt. 8:9). Here was a man who truly knew authority. He could
submit to authority; therefore, he was able to be a deputy authority himself. We have said that God upholds and maintains the
whole universe with His authority. He also begets His children
with His authority (John 1:12) and binds them together with His
authority. Therefore, if a man is independent, individualistic, and
free from any God-appointed deputy authority, he is an outsider
as far as God's administration over the whole universe is concerned. He cannot get along with other children of God, and as
such, he cannot accomplish God's work on earth today. (*CWWN*,
vol. 47, "Authority and Submission," p. 207)

Today's Reading

An elder must not be an arrogant person. If a person becomes
proud as soon as he assumes authority, he is not qualified to be
an elder. An elder in a local church should feel as if he has no
authority at all. If an elder is always conscious of his authority,
he is not qualified to be an elder or to handle the affairs of the
church. Only the foolish and the narrow-minded are proud. Such
ones cannot stand the temptation of God's glory, and they cannot
bear God's commission and assignment. Once such ones are
entrusted with something, they fall into a snare. This is why a
new convert cannot be an overseer (1 Tim. 3:6).

Authority is of God, and we are merely His deputies. All authority belongs to God....We need to live moment by moment in fellowship with Him....We are merely representatives. Authority does not belong to me; therefore, I cannot be subjective. I must live in fellowship. Once fellowship is cut off, authority is gone. Those who are in authority are placed in an awkward position—they cannot quit and they cannot relax....No one who truly knows God would like to be an authority. To be a deputy authority is a great matter; it is a serious thing.

In order to be a deputy authority, we must fulfill the condition of spirituality as well as the condition of humility. The qualification of an authority is based on one's consciousness of his inability and unsuitability. One thing is sure: None of the persons that God used in the Old and New Testaments were proud....We must be conscious of our unprofitableness all the time, because God can only use the unprofitable slaves. We are not saying this to be polite. We honestly should feel that we are unprofitable slaves...We should always stand in the position of a slave (Luke 17:10). God never entrusts His authority to the self-confident and self-assured. We have to reject pride and learn humility and meekness.

Finally the Lord said, "For even the Son of Man did not come to be served, but to serve and to give His life as a ransom for many" (Mark 10:45). The Lord did not come to be an authority but to serve. The less ambition a man has and the more he humbles himself before the Lord, the more useful he is in the eyes of the Lord. The more a man thinks highly of himself and the more he thinks he is different from others, the less he is useful in the hand of the Lord....We should not try to seize any fleshly authority with fleshly hands. We should be the servants of all. Then when God commits certain responsibilities to us, we will learn to represent Him. The basis of authority is ministry, and there is ministry only where there is resurrection. (*CWWN*, vol. 47, "Authority and Submission," pp. 299-300, 218-219, 286-287)

Further Reading: Authority and Submission, chs. 12, 17-20

Enlightenment and inspiration: _____

_____

_____

_____

Hymns, #551

1 I've believed the true report,
  Hallelujah to the Lamb!
I have passed the outer court,
  Oh, glory be to God!
I am all on Jesus' side,
On the altar sanctified,
To the world and sin I've died,
  Hallelujah to the Lamb!

  Hallelujah! Hallelujah!
  I have passed the riven veil,
  Here the glories never fail,
  Hallelujah! Hallelujah!
  I am living in the presence of the King.

2 I'm a king and priest to God,
  Hallelujah to the Lamb!
By the cleansing of the blood,
  Oh, glory be to God!
By the Spirit's pow'r and light,
I am living day and night,
In the holiest place so bright,
  Hallelujah to the Lamb!

3 I have passed the outer veil,
  Hallelujah to the Lamb!
Which did once God's light conceal,
  Oh, glory be to God!
But the blood has brought me in
To God's holiness so clean,
Where there's death to self and sin,
  Hallelujah to the Lamb!

4 I'm within the holiest pale,
  Hallelujah to the Lamb!
I have passed the inner veil,
  Oh, glory be to God!
I am sanctified to God
By the power of the blood,
Now the Lord is my abode,
  Hallelujah to the Lamb!

Composition for prophecy with main point and sub-points: _____

How One Ought to Conduct Himself in the Church in Order to Bring Forth the One New Man

Scripture Reading: 1 Tim. 3:15; Eph. 2:13-16; 3:16-21; Col. 3:10-11; 1 Cor. 12:12-13

Day 1 I. First Timothy 3:15 says, "If I delay, I write that you may know how one ought to conduct himself in the house of God, which is the church of the living God":

A. Here *conduct* refers to administration; Timothy received Paul's commission to arrange for matters related to the administration of the churches.

B. When Paul speaks of knowing "how one ought to conduct himself in the house of God," he is speaking of how to administrate and arrange matters in the church.

C. It may seem that Paul is speaking only about being delayed himself, but if we have spiritual insight, we will realize that he is actually referring to the Lord being delayed; before the Lord comes back, we must know how to administrate the church, how to conduct ourselves in the church.

II. If we want to clearly know what the church is and what God desires to do in the church, so that we may know how we ought to conduct ourselves in the church, we need to understand Ephesians 2:13-16, Colossians 3:10-11, and 1 Corinthians 12:12-13:

A. Ephesians 2 is concerning the Gentiles and the Jews becoming one new man in Christ:

1. The new man does not refer to an individual; the new man is a corporate new man; hence, verse 15 clearly says that Christ created the two (the Jews and the Gentiles) into one new man.

2. Christ broke down the middle wall of partition between the Jews and the Gentiles by
abolishing the law of the commandments in
ordinances; when He was crucified on the
cross, all the ordinances were nailed there
(v. 15; Col. 2:14):

  a. Ordinances refer to the ceremonial law
with its rituals, which are the forms or
ways of living and worship.

  b. These forms or ways of living and worship create enmity and division; to practice the proper church life, all ordinances
should be repudiated and dropped.

Day 2
  3. "And might reconcile both [the Jews and
the Gentiles] in one Body to God through
the cross, having slain the enmity by it"
(Eph. 2:16):

  a. This one Body, the church (1:23), is the
one new man mentioned in the previous
verse, 2:15; it was in this one Body that
both the Jews and the Gentiles were reconciled to God through the cross.

  b. We, the believers, whether Jews or Gen-
tiles, were reconciled not only *for* the
Body of Christ but also *in* the Body of
Christ; what a revelation is here!

  c. We were reconciled to God; we were saved
in the Body of Christ.

4. Before we were saved, we were in Adam, the
old man; when we were saved, we came out
of Adam, put off the old man, and put on
Christ, the new man (Col. 3:9-10; Eph. 2:15).

B. "And have put on the new man, which is being
renewed unto full knowledge according to the
image of Him who created him" (Col. 3:10):

1. Since Christ is the constituent of the new man
(v. 11; 1:27-28), we, who are the new man, are
one with Christ; this is the most basic and crucial point in the book of Colossians.

2. Although we have put on Christ (Gal. 3:27) and Christ is in us (Col. 1:27), the new man has not yet been manifested through us.

3. Because the new man was created with us, who belong to the old creation (Eph. 2:15), as his constituents, he needs to be renewed; this renewing takes place mainly in our mind, as indicated by the phrase *unto full knowledge* in Colossians 3:10.

4. The new man was created in our spirit and is being renewed in our mind unto full knowledge according to the image of Christ, who is the very expression of God (1:15; Heb. 1:3a).

5. As we know the Lord more and more (Phil. 3:8, 10), the new man will be renewed more and more, and the image of the Lord will be manifested more for the bringing forth of the one new man.

C. Colossians 3:11 indicates that Greek and Jew, circumcision and uncircumcision, barbarian, Scythian, slave, and free man are on the cross; *there cannot be* is a strong word indicating that everything has been terminated, that there is no natural person in the new man, and that there cannot be anything in the new man except Christ, who is "all and in all"; if we truly see this light, there will be such a change in our service and work.

Day 3 & Day 4

D. Concerning the Body of Christ, 1 Corinthians 12:12-13 says, "Even as the body is one and has many members, yet all the members of the body, being many, are one body, so also is the Christ. For also in one Spirit we were all baptized into one Body, whether Jews or Greeks, whether slaves or free, and were all given to drink one Spirit":

1. This corresponds to Colossians 3:11; we have all been baptized in the Holy Spirit into one Body, that is, into one new man, into Christ.

2. By the cross and by our passing through the cross, Christ has reconciled His redeemed ones and created them in Himself into one new man.

3. This new man, this Body, is Christ Himself; in this new man there are no differences; there is only Christ; Christ is all the members and in all the members.

E. It is only when we are clear concerning all the points above that we will know how to administrate and serve (how to conduct ourselves) in the church.

III. **We can see ten crucial points in the administration of the church by the pattern of Paul; we should allow the Holy Spirit to inscribe these ten points in the tablets of our heart so that we may live in them (cf. 2 Cor. 3:3):**

A. First, in Galatians 1:15-16 he says that he served God because it pleased God to reveal His Son in him that he might announce Him as the gospel among the Gentiles; Paul announced the living Christ whom God had revealed in him, not knowledge or doctrine (cf. Acts 26:16-19).

B. Second, we must clearly see that Christ is "our life" (Col. 3:4); Christ being our life means that He is the life of the Body, of the new man; furthermore, that Christ is our life is a strong indication that we are to take Him as life and live by Him, that we are to live Him in our daily life in order to experience the universally extensive Christ revealed in Colossians, so that all He is and has attained and obtained will not remain objective but will become our subjective experience.

C. Third, along with Paul, we need to realize that we need to live in Christ; he says, "I...have died to law that I might live to God...And the life which I now live in the flesh I live in faith, the faith of the Son of God, who loved me and gave Himself up for me" (Gal. 2:19-20).

D. Fourth, we need to see that what we are and
have has been terminated on the cross; Paul
says, "I am crucified with Christ; and it is no
longer I who live, but it is Christ who lives in me"
(v. 20).

E. Fifth, we must not serve according to what we
are or what we have in ourselves; in Galatians
6:14 Paul says, "The world has been crucified to
me and I to the world."

F. Sixth, Paul's unique goal, and ours, should be to
dispense Christ into others so that Christ could
increase in them; in Galatians 4:19 he says, "I
travail again in birth until Christ is formed in
you."

G. Seventh, we should not expect those with whom
we serve to change in any way; instead, we
should desire only that they gain Christ, be
filled with Christ, and be fully gained by Christ;
in 1 Corinthians 2:2 Paul says, "I did not deter-
mine to know anything among you except Jesus
Christ, and this One crucified."

H. Eighth, we must clearly see that there should
only be one result in our service, work, and
administration of the church—Christ must be
produced in the church so that everyone has
Christ, so that Christ increases in every member, and so that all will arrive at the measure of
the stature of the fullness of Christ (Eph. 4:13);
in 2 Corinthians 4:12 Paul says, "Death operates in us, but life in you."

I. Ninth, Paul prayed for all these matters (Rom.
1:9; Eph. 1:16; Col. 1:9; 1 Thes. 1:2); we must be
men of prayer (Col. 4:2).

J. Tenth, we must be like the apostle Paul, who
had a living faith, believing that God is able "to
do superabundantly above all that we ask or
think, according to the power which operates in
us" (Eph. 3:20), especially concerning the points
listed above.

Day 5 IV. **Ephesians 3:16-21 reveals the spirit, attitude, prayer, and faith that a serving one should have in order to work out the New Jerusalem and bring forth the one new man:**

A. Paul's spirit and attitude—what he saw, what he was filled with, what he said, and what he cared about in his heart—were related to the vision of God being manifested in the flesh and being mingled with man in order to build the church with Christ so that the church would be filled with Christ; the most precious point in Ephesians 3:16-21 is not Paul's prayer and faith but his spirit and attitude.

B. We should cooperate with Christ so that we can work Christ into others and build Christ as the material into others so that they may become a spiritual temple for the expression, the fullness, of the One who fills all in all—this should be our spirit and attitude.

C. Paul was so burdened that he said, "I bow my knees unto the Father" (v. 14); Paul knelt down to pray because something within forced him to bow his knees unto the Father; because Paul was obsessed with Christ, in Ephesians 3 he could not help but kneel down.

D. Every elder, deacon, co-worker, and everyone who serves the Lord must see a vision, a revelation, to the point that he is absolutely obsessed with it and has the same spirit, attitude, and inner mood of Paul.

E. Paul described four aspects of our need to be strengthened into the inner man by the Father:

1. The first aspect of the strengthening of the believers is that it would be "according to the riches of His glory" (v. 16); God expressed is glory (cf. Exo. 40:34; 2 Chron. 7:3; Ezek. 1:28; 10:4):

   a. What dwells in Christ is the expression of the riches of what God is, and the

glory that is expressed is the fullness
(Col. 2:9; Eph. 3:19b); this means that
God wants to be expressed.

b. God's glory is wrought into the church, and
He is expressed in the church; hence, to
God is the glory in the church (vv. 20-21).

c. The glory of the expressed God can enter
into the believers and become the strengthening power within them; in turn, they
are strengthened to express God's glory.

2. The second aspect of the strengthening of
the believers is "through His Spirit" (v. 16);
without the Spirit, God cannot be expressed
through man; the Father strengthens us
from within through the indwelling Spirit,
who has been with us and in us since our
regeneration.

3. The third aspect of the strengthening of the
believers is that they would be strengthened "with power" (v. 16); this is the power
that is referred to in 1:19-22—the power that
raised Christ from the dead, seated Christ
at the right hand of God in the heavenlies,
subjected all things under Christ's feet, and
gave Christ to be Head over all things to the
church; such power operates in us (vv. 19-20),
and with such power God strengthens us for
the church.

4. The fourth aspect of the strengthening of
the believers is that they would be strengthened "into the inner man" (3:16); the inner
man is our regenerated spirit, which has
God's life as its life; this implies that we need
to be strengthened into our spirit through the
Holy Spirit.

Day 6   F. The issue is Christ making His home in our
hearts; *hearts* in Ephesians 3:17 is an important
word, meaning that Christ can be sensed in us
and that we respond to Christ dwelling in us;

our heart is the organ of our feeling and emotion, and it is where Christ dwells in us:

1. Paul never neglected the need to work Christ
    into man; he was obsessed with the matter
    of Christ increasing in us, which was his
    central concern, and this became his spirit
    and attitude; when Paul wrote Ephesians
    3:16-21, he transcended even the universe.

2. When Christ is in our feeling and is real in
    our heart, we will be rooted and grounded
    in His love; in such a condition Paul said
    that we would apprehend with all the saints
    the breadth, length, height, and depth; these
    four words added together equal Christ in
    His immeasurableness.

3. The result of all this is that we will know
    the knowledge-surpassing love of Christ and
    be filled unto all the fullness of God (v. 19);
    we who serve in the church should have this
    attitude, and our thoughts and prayers should
    be for this.

4. The responsible brothers should be clear as
    to what they take as their goal: is it an in-
    crease in number or an increase in Christ?
    They should be like Paul, who was totally
    obsessed with the increase of Christ within
    God's people.

5. We should focus on this matter to the extent
    that we do not know what to pray other
    than this; this should be the attitude, spirit,
    and prayer of one who serves the Lord.

G. Because Paul was concerned that the Ephesian
    saints might think that the prayer in verses 16
    through 19 was too difficult, he expressed his
    faith by immediately following with verses 20
    and 21—"but to Him who is able to do super-
    abundantly above all that we ask or think, ac-
    cording to the power which operates in us, to
    Him be the glory in the church and in Christ

Jesus unto all the generations forever and ever.
Amen":

1. The full meaning of the phrase *to Him be the
   glory in the church* is seen in the New Jerusalem; the New Jerusalem is the complete
   manifestation of God's glory (Rev. 21:10-11),
   and the church today should be a miniature
   of the New Jerusalem.
2. This is the spirit, attitude, prayer, and faith
   with which we should serve the Lord; in this
   way our service in the church will be great
   and glorious, and the brothers and sisters
   will be filled unto all the fullness of God
   (Eph. 3:19b; cf. Gal. 4:19).

Morning Nourishment

1 Tim. But if I delay, *I write* that you may know how one
3:15   ought to conduct himself in the house of God,
        which is the church of the living God, the pillar
        and base of the truth.
Eph.   For He Himself is our peace, He who has made
2:14-15 both one and has broken down the middle wall of
        partition,...that He might create the two in Him-
        self into one new man, *so* making peace.

We must consider the administration of the church with the
Scriptures as our basis. [In] 1 Timothy 3:15...*conduct* refers to administration. Paul wrote to Timothy, and Timothy received Paul's
commission to arrange for matters related to the management and
administration of the churches. When Paul spoke of knowing "how
one ought to conduct himself in the house of God," he was speaking
of how to administrate and arrange matters in the church. Paul
said this because he knew that he might be absent for a long period
of time, that he might be delayed. Therefore, he wanted Timothy to
know how to administrate the church and how to conduct himself
in the church. It may seem that Paul was speaking only about being delayed himself, but if we have spiritual insight, we will realize
that he was actually referring to the Lord being delayed. Before the
Lord comes back, we must know how to administrate the church
and how to conduct ourselves in the church. This is the only verse
in the entire Bible which clearly speaks of administrating the
church and conducting ourselves in the church. (*How to Administrate the Church,* p. 9)

Today's Reading

If we want to clearly know what the church is and what God
desires to do in the church, we need to understand Ephesians
2:13-16, Colossians 3:10-11, and 1 Corinthians 12:12-13....
Ephesians 2...concerns the Gentiles and the Jews becoming
one new man in Christ.

In Ephesians 2 the apostle shows that these two, who
could not come near and who were far off from one another,

have become one new man in Christ. Thus, verse 13 says, "But now in Christ Jesus you who were once far off have become near in the blood of Christ." *You who were once far off* refers to the Gentiles. The Gentiles were once far off from the Jews, but now through the redemption of Christ with the shedding of His blood, they have come near to the Jews. Verse 14 says, "For He Himself is our peace, He who has made both one and has broken down the middle wall of partition, the enmity."... Christ accomplished redemption on the cross so that both— the Gentiles and the Jews—could become one. He also broke down the middle wall of partition. What is "the middle wall of partition"? Verse 15 says, "Abolishing in His flesh the law of the commandments in ordinances, that He might create the two in Himself into one new man, so making peace." The middle wall of partition is the law of the commandments in ordinances. The law does not allow the Jews to have any deal- ings with the Gentiles, and because of this, there was a middle wall, there was enmity. But Christ crucified the law and abol- ished the enmity on the cross so that He might create the two in Himself into one new man. Christ has created the two in Himself into one new man.

In the New Testament the *new man* does not refer to an indi- vidual; there is no individual new man. The new man is a corpo- rate new man. In other words, in the New Testament there is only one new man, not many new men, just as there is only one old man, not many old men (cf. Gen. 1:26; 1 Cor. 15:47)....Hence, Ephesians 2:15 clearly says that Christ created "the two in Him- self into one new man." *The two* refers to the Gentiles and the Jews. Formerly, they were separated by the law, but now the middle wall of partition has been broken down through the cru- cifixion of Christ. Thus, the two were created in Christ into one new man. (*How to Administrate the Church*, pp. 103-104)

Further Reading: How to Administrate the Church, ch. 1; *CWWN*, vol. 44, "The Mystery of Christ," ch. 1

Enlightenment and inspiration: _____

_____

_____

_____

Morning Nourishment

Eph.	And might reconcile both in one Body to God
2:16	through the cross, having slain the enmity by it.
Col.	And have put on the new man, which is being
3:10-11	renewed unto full knowledge according to the image of Him who created him, where there cannot be Greek and Jew, circumcision and uncircumcision, barbarian, Scythian, slave, free man, but Christ is all and in all.

Ephesians 2:16...clearly shows that through the cross Christ broke down the middle wall of partition between the Jews and the Gentiles in the old creation and created the two in Himself into one new man; as a result, the two are one Body. Formerly there were Jews and Gentiles, but now the two have been created in Christ into one new man. (*How to Administrate the Church*, p. 104)

This one Body, the church (Eph. 1:23), is the one new man mentioned in 2:15. It was in this one Body that both the Jews and the Gentiles were reconciled to God through the cross. We, the believers, whether Jews or Gentiles, were reconciled not only *for* the Body of Christ but also *in* the Body of Christ. What a revelation here! We were reconciled to God; we were saved in the Body of Christ. (Eph. 2:16, footnote 2)

Today's Reading

[Verses 9 and 10 of Colossians 3] are not a charge that we put off the old man and put on the new man; rather, they refer to an accomplished fact. In Christ, we have put off the old man and put on the new man. We must read Colossians 3:10 with Ephesians 2:15, which says that Christ has created the Gentiles and the Jews in Himself into one new man; Colossians says that in Christ the old man has been put off, and the new man has been put on.

To put on the new man does not mean that you put on a new man, I put on a new man, and millions of believers put on millions of new men....There is only one new man. The old man is Adam; the new man is Christ. Before we were saved, we were in Adam, the old man; when we were saved, we came out of Adam, put off the old man, and put on Christ, the new man. (*How to Administrate the Church,* pp. 104-105)

Since Christ is the constituent of the new man, we, who are the new man, are one with Christ. This is the most basic and crucial point in Colossians. (Col. 3:10, footnote 2)

Because the new man was created with us, who belong to the old creation (Eph. 2:15), as his constituents, he needs to be renewed. This renewing takes place mainly in our mind, as indicated by the phrase *unto full knowledge.* The new man was created in our spirit and is being renewed in our mind unto full knowledge according to the image of Christ. (Col. 3:10, footnote 3)

Although we have put on Christ and Christ is in us, the new man has not yet been manifested through us. According to Colossians 3:10, the new man "is being renewed unto full knowledge." When we are saved, Christ enters into us and we put Him on (Gal. 3:27). However, we do not have sufficient knowledge of Christ. Thus, from the day of our salvation, we are being renewed unto full knowledge. The more we believe, the more knowledge we receive; the more we believe, the more thorough our knowledge becomes; and the more we believe, the fuller our knowledge will be.

Colossians 3:11 indicates that Greek and Jew, circumcision and uncircumcision, barbarian, Scythian, slave, and free man are on the cross. Everyone is on the cross. You are on the cross, and I am on the cross. There is no natural person in the new man. *There cannot be* is a strong word indicating that everything has been terminated. There cannot be anything in the new man except Christ, who is "all and in all." There cannot be Southerners and Northerners, educated and uneducated, in the church; there is only Christ. There cannot be you or me, and there cannot be slave or free, but Christ is all.

In the church there is only Christ; in the church Christ is all and in all. If we truly see this light, there will be such a change in our service and work! (*How to Administrate the Church,* pp. 105-106)

Further Reading: How to Administrate the Church, ch. 8

Enlightenment and inspiration: _____

_____

_____

_____

Morning Nourishment

1 Cor. **For even as the body is one and has many mem-**
12:12-13 **bers, yet all the members of the body, being many,**
are one body, so also is the Christ. For also in one
Spirit we were all baptized into one Body, whether
Jews or Greeks, whether slaves or free, and were
all given to drink one Spirit.

[In 1 Corinthians 12:12, a verse concerning the Body of Christ], the clause *so also is the Christ* indicates that the church is Christ. Verse 13 continues, "For also in one Spirit we were all baptized into one Body, whether Jews or Greeks, whether slaves or free, and were all given to drink one Spirit." This corresponds to Colossians 3:11. Whether we are Jews or Greeks, whether we are slaves or free, we have all been baptized in one Spirit into one Body, and this Body is Christ. We have all been baptized in the Holy Spirit into one Body, that is, into one new man, into Christ.

Formerly, we were outside of the cross and in the old man, in Adam. In Adam, in our old man, there are many differences. There are Gentiles and Jews, Southerners and Northerners, educated and uneducated, slaves and free. Nevertheless, the cross has dealt with all these differences. On the cross all things in the universe have been terminated. The cross can abolish enmity and every kind of difference because the cross abolished all of the old creation and everything in it. By the cross and by our passing through the cross, Christ has reconciled His redeemed ones and created them in Himself into one new man. (*How to Administrate the Church*, p. 107)

Today's Reading

In this new man there is only Christ; He is all and in all. Although there are many members in this new man, there is only one Body. In 1 Corinthians 12 those who are Jews, Gentiles, slaves, or free have all been baptized in the Holy Spirit into one Body, into the one new man. This new man, this Body, is Christ Himself; in this new man there are no differences; there is only Christ. Christ is all and in all.

From the various portions of the Word above, we can see what the church is. All of the serving ones in the church must see what the church is, what the nature of the church is, what God intends to build, and with what God builds the church. Only when we are clear concerning all these points can we administrate and serve in the church.

First, in order to administrate in the church, we must have Christ revealed in us. Second, we must clearly see that Christ is our life. Third, we should realize that we must live in Christ. Fourth, we must see that what we are and what we have in ourselves has been terminated on the cross. Fifth, we must not serve or work according to what we are and what we have in ourselves. Sixth, we should not dispense anything other than Christ in our service and work in the church. Seventh, we should not expect those with whom we serve to change in any way; instead, we should desire only that they gain Christ, be filled with Christ, and be fully gained by Christ. Eighth, we must clearly see that there should be only one result in our service, work, and administration of the church. Christ must be produced in the church so that everyone has Christ, so that Christ increases in every member, and so that all will arrive at the measure of the stature of the fullness of Christ. Ninth, in order to administrate the church, we must pray for the above eight points; we must be men of prayer. Tenth, we must be like the apostle Paul who had a living faith, believing that God can accomplish these points. The first eight points constitute proper service in the administration of the church; the last two points state that we must pray and have faith, praying for the above eight points every day, believing that God is able to do superabundantly above all that we ask or think. The power of God is not outside of us but inside of us. Through the operation of the power within us, God can fulfill all these things. This is the administration of the church. If we do not see this, our service in the church will be null and void. (*How to Administrate the Church,* pp. 107-108)

Further Reading: How to Administrate the Church, ch. 9

Enlightenment and inspiration: _____

_____

_____

_____

Morning Nourishment

Gal. **But when it pleased God, who set me apart from**
1:15-16 **my mother's womb and called me through His**
grace, to reveal His Son in me that I might an-
nounce Him as the gospel among the Gentiles, im-
mediately I did not confer with flesh and blood.

In his fourteen Epistles, Paul clearly speaks of these [fol-
lowing] ten points.

First, in Galatians 1:15-16 he says that he...served God in
such a way because God revealed His Son in him so that he
might announce Christ among the Gentiles. He announced the
Son of God....Paul announced the living Christ whom God had
revealed in him, not knowledge or doctrine.

Second, in Colossians 3:4 Paul speaks of "Christ our life," indicating that he lived in God together with Christ. Third, to those
who tried to work out the law by themselves, he says, "I...have died
to law that I might live to God,...and the life which I now live in the
flesh I live in faith, the faith of the Son of God, who loved me and
gave Himself up for me" (Gal. 2:19-20). He realized that he needed
to live in Christ. Fourth, Paul says, "I am crucified with Christ; and
it is no longer I who live, but it is Christ who lives in me" (v. 20). This
means that he realized that all that he had was terminated on the
cross. Fifth, in Galatians 6:14 he says, "The world has been crucified to me and I to the world." This means that he knew that he was
terminated and that he lived in Christ. With respect to the cross,
Paul was finished; he no longer lived according to his former self.
Not only did Paul feel this way, but even those in the world saw him
in this way. (*How to Administrate the Church*, pp. 108-110)

Today's Reading

Sixth, in Galatians 4:19 he says, "I travail again in birth until
Christ is formed in you." Paul's unique goal was to dispense
Christ into others so that Christ could increase in them.

Seventh, in 1 Corinthians 2:2 Paul says, "I did not...know anything among you except Jesus Christ, and this One crucified." At
that time there were many problems in the church in Corinth;

some of the saints were fleshy, some were fleshly, and some had sinned. Paul did not expect those who were cold to become more fervent or those who were wrong to improve; rather, he had only one hope, the hope that Christ would increase in them. Among the believers in Corinth, some were fervent toward the Jewish religion, some sought signs, some sought philosophical knowledge, and some even sought spiritual gifts, but Paul preached Christ crucified. He did not care about gifts and signs; he hoped only for the increase of Christ in them.

Eighth, in 2 Corinthians 4:12, Paul says, "Death operates in us, but life in you." Paul saw that the result of his work could only be Christ and life. If he saw that the result of others' work was not Christ, he would write to admonish and adjust them (1 Cor. 4:14). The unique purpose of his fourteen Epistles was to bring man into Christ and to cause the measure of the stature of the fullness of Christ to grow in the church (Eph. 4:13). This was his only expectation. Ninth, Paul prayed for all these matters (Rom. 1:9; Eph. 1:16; Col. 1:9; 1 Thes. 1:2). Tenth, he believed that God was able to do above all that he asked or thought (Eph. 3:20).

These ten points can be summed up in one point—Christ. Paul saw Christ. He announced Christ. His work was Christ. He prayed Christ. His faith was Christ. And the result of his work, all the more, was Christ. From beginning to end, Christ was central. Christ passed through Paul and reached all those whom he served; that is, Christ was produced in them.

We should be people of the New Testament, allowing the Holy Spirit to inscribe these ten points onto the tablets of our heart so that we may live in them. This is the administration of the church, the service in the church; this is the purpose of our visiting people, preaching the gospel, and edifying others. All the elders, deacons, and those who serve in the church should follow this pattern. (*How to Administrate the Church,* pp. 110-111)

Further Reading: The Way to Build Up the Church (booklet); *Life-study of Ephesians,* msg. 32

Enlightenment and inspiration: _____

_____

_____

_____

Morning Nourishment

Eph. **That He would grant you, according to the riches of**
3:16-18 **His glory, to be strengthened with power through**
His Spirit into the inner man, that Christ may make
His home in your hearts through faith, that you,
being rooted and grounded in love, may be full of
strength to apprehend with all the saints what the
breadth and length and height and depth are.

Ephesians 3:16-21...helps us know how to serve God in the
church and shows Paul's spirit, attitude, prayer, and faith. We
should have this spirit, attitude, prayer, and faith when we serve
God in the church.

Paul's spirit and attitude—what he saw, what he was filled
with, what he said, and what he cared about in his heart—were
related to the vision of God being manifested in the flesh and
being mingled with man in order to build the church with Christ
so that the church would be filled with Christ....The most precious point in this portion of the Scriptures is not Paul's prayer
and faith but his spirit and attitude. After...seeing the church
and the building material of the church, we should become so captivated and enthralled that we are eager to return to our locality.
We should return so that we can work Christ into others and
build Christ as the material into others so that they may become
a spiritual temple for the expression of the fullness of the One
who fills all in all. This should be our spirit and attitude. (*How to*
Administrate the Church, pp. 117-119)

Today's Reading

Paul knelt down to pray because he was so burdened; something heavy within forced him to bow his knees unto the Father.
His vision, his revelation, and his seeing became his spirit, his
attitude, and his inner mood....Because Paul was "obsessed" with
Christ, in Ephesians 3 he could not help but kneel down.

Every elder, deacon, co-worker, and everyone who serves the
Lord must see a vision, a revelation, to the point that he is absolutely obsessed with it and has the same spirit, attitude, and

mood of Paul. Because Paul had such a spirit, attitude, and mood, he spontaneously had this kind of prayer; he also believed that God is able to do superabundantly. All those who serve God in the church must have this kind of spirit and attitude and this kind of prayer. All of our prayers must take this kind of prayer as the center, and we should have the faith for such prayer.

In Paul's prayer, he asked that God would grant the Ephesian believers to be strengthened....He described four aspects of this strengthening. First, he prayed that it would be "according to the riches of His glory" (v. 16). What is glory? Glory is the expression of the mystery, the content within God. In the Bible, *glory* refers to God being expressed. God expressed is glory.

Since glory is God expressed, "the riches of His glory" must refer to the expression of the riches of God's life and nature, the riches of His excellent attributes, the riches of the Godhead.... Colossians 2:9 speaks of all the fullness of the Godhead, which refers to the expression of God's riches.

Paul...prayed that the riches of God's glory would enter into the believers so that they would be strengthened to an extent that others could sense God's expression. The glory of the expressed God can enter into the believers and become the strengthening power within them. In turn, they are strengthened to express God's glory.

The second aspect of the strengthening of the Ephesian believers is "through His Spirit." Without the Spirit, God cannot be expressed through man. The third aspect is that the Ephesian believers would be strengthened "with power" into the inner man. This means that God's power enters into man and becomes a motivating power to strengthen man. The fourth aspect is that they would be strengthened "into the inner man."...The purpose of this strengthening is that we may express God's glory, which is God Himself. (*How to Administrate the Church*, pp. 119-122)

Further Reading: CWWL, 1970, vol. 2, "The Two Greatest Prayers of the Apostle Paul," chs. 3-4

Enlightenment and inspiration: _____

_____

_____

_____

Morning Nourishment

Eph. And to know the knowledge-surpassing love of
3:19-21 Christ, that you may be filled unto all the fullness
of God. But to Him who is able to do superabundantly above all that we ask or think, according to
the power which operates in us, to Him be the
glory in the church and in Christ Jesus unto all the
generations forever and ever. Amen.

Paul did not speak of Christ earlier; he only spoke of glory
and the Spirit, but the issue is Christ making His home in our
hearts [Eph. 3:17]....[Galatians 4:19] says, "Until Christ is formed
in you." This refers to Christ's making His home in our hearts.
Hearts in Ephesians 3:17 is an important word, meaning that
Christ can be sensed in us. He not only dwells in us, but He
dwells in our heart,...the organ of our feeling and emotion. (*How
to Administrate the Church,* p. 122)

Today's Reading

Paul never neglected the need to work Christ into man....It
seemed that Paul was "obsessed" with the matter of Christ in us,
and this became his spirit and attitude. Paul knew that Christ was
not in the hearts of the Ephesian believers, even though He was in
them....Paul's central concern was related to Christ's being in the
believers. In our work and service of administrating the church, we
should have this kind of spirit, expecting that the believers will
have Christ in them and that Christ will enter into them.

When he was writing [Ephesians 3], Paul transcended even the
universe....When Christ is in our feeling and is real in our heart, we
will be rooted and grounded in His love. In such a condition, Paul
said that we would know the breadth, the length, the height, and
the depth....What are the breadth, the length, the height, and the
depth? These four words added together equal immeasurableness....If we know Christ inwardly, live in Him, and are rooted and
grounded in His love, we will see that the One who dwells in us is
the breadth, the length, the height, and the depth.

Paul continued in 3:19, "And to know the knowledge-surpassing love of Christ," the result of which is "that you may be filled unto all the fullness of God." Paul was entirely captivated by this matter, and it became his spirit and attitude. When Christ has made His home in our hearts, we can apprehend His immeasurableness, and the result is that we are filled unto all the fullness of God. We who serve in the church should have this attitude, and our thoughts and prayers should be for this.

In administrating the church, all the responsible brothers must take this as their spirit, their attitude, and their hope. They should not hope merely that all the saints will come to the meetings, be zealous, preach the gospel, and bring people to salvation. The responsible brothers should be clear as to what they take as their goal: is it an increase in numbers or an increase in Christ? They should be like Paul, who was totally "obsessed" with this matter.

We should focus on this matter to the extent that we do not know what to pray other than this....This should be the attitude, spirit, and prayer of one who serves God.

Because Paul was concerned that the Ephesian saints might think that the prayer in verses 16 through 19 was too difficult, he immediately followed with verse 20, saying, God is "able" and "above all that we ask or think." In the end, he praised God for being glorified in the church and in Christ Jesus. *Glory* in verse 21 means that God is greatly released and expressed in the church; this is glory....The full meaning of the phrase *to Him be the glory in the church* is seen in the New Jerusalem. On that day, God will shine forth all of His fullness....The New Jerusalem is the complete expression of God's glory; the church today should be a miniature of the New Jerusalem. This is the spirit, attitude, prayer, and faith with which we should serve the Lord....Our spirit and attitude should be that the brothers and sisters will have Christ inwardly, that Christ will make His home in their hearts, and that they will be filled unto all the fullness of God. (*How to Administrate the Church*, pp. 122-127)

Further Reading: Life-study of Ephesians, msgs. 33-35

Enlightenment and inspiration: _____

_____

_____

_____

Hymns, #1232

1   Once by nature we were dead in sin,
    In a world of utter discord;
    But together God has quickened us,
    Raised us up to sit together with the Lord.

      Jesus is getting us together,
      Come and see the saints in one accord.
      His love is knitting us together,
      To the stature of the fullness of the Lord.

2   Thus with all saints we can apprehend
    All the vast dimensions of God.
    Knowing Christ's love passes all we know.
    We're together filled to fullness with our God.

3   Now we know the purpose of our God,
    Visible the mystery became:
    Christ, the church, together now we see,
    And together put the enemy to shame.

4   For this cause we pray the Father God—
    Strengthen Thou with might our inner man;
    Make Yourself at home in all our hearts,
    Root us, ground us in Your love and for
      Your plan.

5   In the Body we'll be fitly framed
    As the many members Christ supply;
    Working in the measure of each part,
    All by growth in love the Body edify.

6   Now we're one His purpose to fulfill,
    As the one new man of His plan.
    Unto Him be glory in the church,
    And in Jesus Christ forevermore—Amen!

Composition for prophecy with main point and sub-points: _____

_____
_____
_____
_____
_____
_____
_____
_____
_____
_____
_____
_____
_____
_____
_____
_____
_____
_____
_____
_____
_____
_____
_____
_____
_____
_____
_____
_____
_____
_____
_____
_____
_____
_____
_____
_____
_____
_____
_____
_____

Reading Schedule for the Recovery Version of the Old Testament with Footnotes

Wk.	Lord's Day	Monday	Tuesday	Wednesday	Thursday	Friday	Saturday
1	Gen. 1:1-5	1:6-23	1:24-31	2:1-9	2:10-25	3:1-13	3:14-24
2	4:1-26	5:1-32	6:1-22	7:1—8:3	8:4-22	9:1-29	10:1-32
3	11:1-32	12:1-20	13:1-18	14:1-24	15:1-21	16:1-16	17:1-27
4	18:1-33	19:1-38	20:1-18	21:1-34	22:1-24	23:1—24:27	24:28-67
5	25:1-34	26:1-35	27:1-46	28:1-22	29:1-35	30:1-43	31:1-55
6	32:1-32	33:1—34:31	35:1-29	36:1-43	37:1-36	38:1—39:23	40:1—41:13
7	41:14-57	42:1-38	43:1-34	44:1-34	45:1-28	46:1-34	47:1-31
8	48:1-22	49:1-15	49:16-33	50:1-26	Exo. 1:1-22	2:1-25	3:1-22
9	4:1-31	5:1-23	6:1-30	7:1-25	8:1-32	9:1-35	10:1-29
10	11:1-10	12:1-14	12:15-36	12:37-51	13:1-22	14:1-31	15:1-27
11	16:1-36	17:1-16	18:1-27	19:1-25	20:1-26	21:1-36	22:1-31
12	23:1-33	24:1-18	25:1-22	25:23-40	26:1-14	26:15-37	27:1-21
13	28:1-21	28:22-43	29:1-21	29:22-46	30:1-10	30:11-38	31:1-17
14	31:18—32:35	33:1-23	34:1-35	35:1-35	36:1-38	37:1-29	38:1-31
15	39:1-43	40:1-38	Lev. 1:1-17	2:1-16	3:1-17	4:1-35	5:1-19
16	6:1-30	7:1-38	8:1-36	9:1-24	10:1-20	11:1-47	12:1-8
17	13:1-28	13:29-59	14:1-18	14:19-32	14:33-57	15:1-33	16:1-17
18	16:18-34	17:1-16	18:1-30	19:1-37	20:1-27	21:1-24	22:1-33
19	23:1-22	23:23-44	24:1-23	25:1-23	25:24-55	26:1-24	26:25-46
20	27:1-34	Num. 1:1-54	2:1-34	3:1-51	4:1-49	5:1-31	6:1-27
21	7:1-41	7:42-88	7:89—8:26	9:1-23	10:1-36	11:1-35	12:1—13:33
22	14:1-45	15:1-41	16:1-50	17:1—18:7	18:8-32	19:1-22	20:1-29
23	21:1-35	22:1-41	23:1-30	24:1-25	25:1-18	26:1-65	27:1-23
24	28:1-31	29:1-40	30:1—31:24	31:25-54	32:1-42	33:1-56	34:1-29
25	35:1-34	36:1-13	Deut. 1:1-46	2:1-37	3:1-29	4:1-49	5:1-33
26	6:1—7:26	8:1-20	9:1-29	10:1-22	11:1-32	12:1-32	13:1—14:21

Reading Schedule for the Recovery Version of the Old Testament with Footnotes

Wk.	Lord's Day	Monday	Tuesday	Wednesday	Thursday	Friday	Saturday
27	14:22—15:23 ☐	16:1-22 ☐	17:1—18:8 ☐	18:9—19:21 ☐	20:1—21:17 ☐	21:18—22:30 ☐	23:1-25 ☐
28	24:1-22 ☐	25:1-19 ☐	26:1-19 ☐	27:1-26 ☐	28:1-68 ☐	29:1-29 ☐	30:1—31:29 ☐
29	31:30—32:52 ☐	33:1-29 ☐	34:1-12 ☐	Josh. 1:1-18 ☐	2:1-24 ☐	3:1-17 ☐	4:1-24 ☐
30	5:1-15 ☐	6:1-27 ☐	7:1-26 ☐	8:1-35 ☐	9:1-27 ☐	10:1-43 ☐	11:1—12:24 ☐
31	13:1-33 ☐	14:1—15:63 ☐	16:1—18:28 ☐	19:1-51 ☐	20:1—21:45 ☐	22:1-34 ☐	23:1—24:33 ☐
32	Judg. 1:1-36 ☐	2:1-23 ☐	3:1-31 ☐	4:1-24 ☐	5:1-31 ☐	6:1-40 ☐	7:1-25 ☐
33	8:1-35 ☐	9:1-57 ☐	10:1—11:40 ☐	12:1—13:25 ☐	14:1—15:20 ☐	16:1-31 ☐	17:1—18:31 ☐
34	19:1-30 ☐	20:1-48 ☐	21:1-25 ☐	Ruth 1:1-22 ☐	2:1-23 ☐	3:1-18 ☐	4:1-22 ☐
35	1 Sam. 1:1-28 ☐	2:1-36 ☐	3:1—4:22 ☐	5:1—6:21 ☐	7:1—8:22 ☐	9:1-27 ☐	10:1—11:15 ☐
36	12:1—13:23 ☐	14:1-52 ☐	15:1-35 ☐	16:1-23 ☐	17:1-58 ☐	18:1-30 ☐	19:1-24 ☐
37	20:1-42 ☐	21:1—22:23 ☐	23:1—24:22 ☐	25:1-44 ☐	26:1-25 ☐	27:1—28:25 ☐	29:1—30:31 ☐
38	31:1-13 ☐	2 Sam. 1:1-27 ☐	2:1-32 ☐	3:1-39 ☐	4:1—5:25 ☐	6:1-23 ☐	7:1-29 ☐
39	8:1—9:13 ☐	10:1—11:27 ☐	12:1-31 ☐	13:1-39 ☐	14:1-33 ☐	15:1—16:23 ☐	17:1—18:33 ☐
40	19:1-43 ☐	20:1—21:22 ☐	22:1-51 ☐	23:1-39 ☐	24:1-25 ☐	1 Kings 1:1-19 ☐	1:20-53 ☐
41	2:1-46 ☐	3:1-28 ☐	4:1-34 ☐	5:1—6:38 ☐	7:1-22 ☐	7:23-51 ☐	8:1-36 ☐
42	8:37-66 ☐	9:1-28 ☐	10:1-29 ☐	11:1-43 ☐	12:1-33 ☐	13:1-34 ☐	14:1-31 ☐
43	15:1-34 ☐	16:1—17:24 ☐	18:1-46 ☐	19:1-21 ☐	20:1-43 ☐	21:1—22:53 ☐	2 Kings 1:1-18 ☐
44	2:1—3:27 ☐	4:1-44 ☐	5:1—6:33 ☐	7:1-20 ☐	8:1-29 ☐	9:1-37 ☐	10:1-36 ☐
45	11:1—12:21 ☐	13:1—14:29 ☐	15:1-38 ☐	16:1-20 ☐	17:1-41 ☐	18:1-37 ☐	19:1-37 ☐
46	20:1—21:26 ☐	22:1-20 ☐	23:1-37 ☐	24:1—25:30 ☐	1 Chron. 1:1-54 ☐	2:1—3:24 ☐	4:1—5:26 ☐
47	6:1-81 ☐	7:1-40 ☐	8:1-40 ☐	9:1-44 ☐	10:1—11:47 ☐	12:1-40 ☐	13:1—14:17 ☐
48	15:1—16:43 ☐	17:1-27 ☐	18:1—19:19 ☐	20:1—21:30 ☐	22:1—23:32 ☐	24:1—25:31 ☐	26:1-32 ☐
49	27:1-34 ☐	28:1—29:30 ☐	2 Chron. 1:1-17 ☐	2:1—3:17 ☐	4:1—5:14 ☐	6:1-42 ☐	7:1—8:18 ☐
50	9:1—10:19 ☐	11:1—12:16 ☐	13:1—15:19 ☐	16:1—17:19 ☐	18:1—19:11 ☐	20:1-37 ☐	21:1—22:12 ☐
51	23:1—24:27 ☐	25:1—26:23 ☐	27:1—28:27 ☐	29:1-36 ☐	30:1—31:21 ☐	32:1-33 ☐	33:1—34:33 ☐
52	35:1—36:23 ☐	Ezra 1:1-11 ☐	2:1-70 ☐	3:1—4:24 ☐	5:1—6:22 ☐	7:1-28 ☐	8:1-36 ☐

Reading Schedule for the Recovery Version of the Old Testament with Footnotes

Wk.	Lord's Day	Monday	Tuesday	Wednesday	Thursday	Friday	Saturday
53	9:1—10:44 ☐	Neh. 1:1-11 ☐	2:1—3:32 ☐	4:1—5:19 ☐	6:1-19 ☐	7:1-73 ☐	8:1-18 ☐
54	9:1-20 ☐	9:21-38 ☐	10:1—11:36 ☐	12:1-47 ☐	13:1-31 ☐	Esth. 1:1-22 ☐	2:1—3:15 ☐
55	4:1—5:14 ☐	6:1—7:10 ☐	8:1-17 ☐	9:1—10:3 ☐	Job 1:1-22 ☐	2:1—3:26 ☐	4:1—5:27 ☐
56	6:1—7:21 ☐	8:1—9:35 ☐	10:1—11:20 ☐	12:1—13:28 ☐	14:1—15:35 ☐	16:1—17:16 ☐	18:1—19:29 ☐
57	20:1—21:34 ☐	22:1—23:17 ☐	24:1—25:6 ☐	26:1—27:23 ☐	28:1—29:25 ☐	30:1—31:40 ☐	32:1—33:33 ☐
58	34:1—35:16 ☐	36:1-33 ☐	37:1-24 ☐	38:1-41 ☐	39:1-30 ☐	40:1-24 ☐	41:1-34 ☐
59	42:1-17 ☐	Psa. 1:1-6 ☐	2:1—3:8 ☐	4:1—6:10 ☐	7:1—8:9 ☐	9:1—10:18 ☐	11:1—15:5 ☐
60	16:1—17:15 ☐	18:1-50 ☐	19:1—21:13 ☐	22:1-31 ☐	23:1—24:10 ☐	25:1—27:14 ☐	28:1—30:12 ☐
61	31:1—32:11 ☐	33:1—34:22 ☐	35:1—36:12 ☐	37:1-40 ☐	38:1—39:13 ☐	40:1—41:13 ☐	42:1—43:5 ☐
62	44:1-26 ☐	45:1-17 ☐	46:1—48:14 ☐	49:1—50:23 ☐	51:1—52:9 ☐	53:1—55:23 ☐	56:1—58:11 ☐
63	59:1—61:8 ☐	62:1—64:10 ☐	65:1—67:7 ☐	68:1-35 ☐	69:1—70:5 ☐	71:1—72:20 ☐	73:1—74:23 ☐
64	75:1—77:20 ☐	78:1-72 ☐	79:1—81:16 ☐	82:1—84:12 ☐	85:1—87:7 ☐	88:1—89:52 ☐	90:1—91:16 ☐
65	92:1—94:23 ☐	95:1—97:12 ☐	98:1—101:8 ☐	102:1—103:22 ☐	104:1—105:45 ☐	106:1-48 ☐	107:1-43 ☐
66	108:1—109:31 ☐	110:1—112:10 ☐	113:1—115:18 ☐	116:1—118:29 ☐	119:1-32 ☐	119:33-72 ☐	119:73-120 ☐
67	119:121-176 ☐	120:1—124:8 ☐	125:1—128:6 ☐	129:1—132:18 ☐	133:1—135:21 ☐	136:1—138:8 ☐	139:1—140:13 ☐
68	141:1—144:15 ☐	145:1—147:20 ☐	148:1—150:6 ☐	Prov. 1:1-33 ☐	2:1—3:35 ☐	4:1—5:23 ☐	6:1-35 ☐
69	7:1—8:36 ☐	9:1—10:32 ☐	11:1—12:28 ☐	13:1—14:35 ☐	15:1-33 ☐	16:1-33 ☐	17:1-28 ☐
70	18:1-24 ☐	19:1—20:30 ☐	21:1—22:29 ☐	23:1-35 ☐	24:1—25:28 ☐	26:1—27:27 ☐	28:1—29:27 ☐
71	30:1-33 ☐	31:1-31 ☐	Eccl. 1:1-18 ☐	2:1—3:22 ☐	4:1—5:20 ☐	6:1—7:29 ☐	8:1—9:18 ☐
72	10:1—11:10 ☐	12:1-14 ☐	S.S. 1:1-8 ☐	1:9-17 ☐	2:1-17 ☐	3:1-11 ☐	4:1-8 ☐
73	4:9-16 ☐	5:1-16 ☐	6:1-13 ☐	7:1-13 ☐	8:1-14 ☐	Isa. 1:1-11 ☐	1:12-31 ☐
74	2:1-22 ☐	3:1-26 ☐	4:1-6 ☐	5:1-30 ☐	6:1-13 ☐	7:1-25 ☐	8:1-22 ☐
75	9:1-21 ☐	10:1-34 ☐	11:1—12:6 ☐	13:1-22 ☐	14:1-14 ☐	14:15-32 ☐	15:1—16:14 ☐
76	17:1—18:7 ☐	19:1-25 ☐	20:1—21:17 ☐	22:1-25 ☐	23:1-18 ☐	24:1-23 ☐	25:1-12 ☐
77	26:1-21 ☐	27:1-13 ☐	28:1-29 ☐	29:1-24 ☐	30:1-33 ☐	31:1—32:20 ☐	33:1-24 ☐
78	34:1-17 ☐	35:1-10 ☐	36:1-22 ☐	37:1-38 ☐	38:1—39:8 ☐	40:1-31 ☐	41:1-29 ☐

Reading Schedule for the Recovery Version of the Old Testament with Footnotes

Wk.	Lord's Day	Monday	Tuesday	Wednesday	Thursday	Friday	Saturday
79	42:1-25 ☐	43:1-28 ☐	44:1-28 ☐	45:1-25 ☐	46:1-13 ☐	47:1-15 ☐	48:1-22 ☐
80	49:1-13 ☐	49:14-26 ☐	50:1—51:23 ☐	52:1-15 ☐	53:1-12 ☐	54:1-17 ☐	55:1-13 ☐
81	56:1-12 ☐	57:1-21 ☐	58:1-14 ☐	59:1-21 ☐	60:1-22 ☐	61:1-11 ☐	62:1-12 ☐
82	63:1-19 ☐	64:1-12 ☐	65:1-25 ☐	66:1-24 ☐	Jer. 1:1-19 ☐	2:1-19 ☐	2:20-37 ☐
83	3:1-25 ☐	4:1-31 ☐	5:1-31 ☐	6:1-30 ☐	7:1-34 ☐	8:1-22 ☐	9:1-26 ☐
84	10:1-25 ☐	11:1—12:17 ☐	13:1-27 ☐	14:1-22 ☐	15:1-21 ☐	16:1—17:27 ☐	18:1-23 ☐
85	19:1—20:18 ☐	21:1—22:30 ☐	23:1-40 ☐	24:1—25:38 ☐	26:1—27:22 ☐	28:1—29:32 ☐	30:1-24 ☐
86	31:1-23 ☐	31:24-40 ☐	32:1-44 ☐	33:1-26 ☐	34:1-22 ☐	35:1-19 ☐	36:1-32 ☐
87	37:1-21 ☐	38:1-28 ☐	39:1—40:16 ☐	41:1—42:22 ☐	43:1—44:30 ☐	45:1—46:28 ☐	47:1—48:16 ☐
88	48:17-47 ☐	49:1-22 ☐	49:23-39 ☐	50:1-27 ☐	50:28-46 ☐	51:1-27 ☐	51:28-64 ☐
89	52:1-34 ☐	Lam. 1:1-22 ☐	2:1-22 ☐	3:1-39 ☐	3:40-66 ☐	4:1-22 ☐	5:1-22 ☐
90	Ezek. 1:1-14 ☐	1:15-28 ☐	2:1—3:27 ☐	4:1—5:17 ☐	6:1—7:27 ☐	8:1—9:11 ☐	10:1—11:25 ☐
91	12:1—13:23 ☐	14:1—15:8 ☐	16:1-63 ☐	17:1—18:32 ☐	19:1-14 ☐	20:1-49 ☐	21:1-32 ☐
92	22:1-31 ☐	23:1-49 ☐	24:1-27 ☐	25:1—26:21 ☐	27:1-36 ☐	28:1-26 ☐	29:1—30:26 ☐
93	31:1—32:32 ☐	33:1-33 ☐	34:1-31 ☐	35:1—36:21 ☐	36:22-38 ☐	37:1-28 ☐	38:1—39:29 ☐
94	40:1-27 ☐	40:28-49 ☐	41:1-26 ☐	42:1—43:27 ☐	44:1-31 ☐	45:1-25 ☐	46:1-24 ☐
95	47:1-23 ☐	48:1-35 ☐	Dan. 1:1-21 ☐	2:1-30 ☐	2:31-49 ☐	3:1-30 ☐	4:1-37 ☐
96	5:1-31 ☐	6:1-28 ☐	7:1-12 ☐	7:13-28 ☐	8:1-27 ☐	9:1-27 ☐	10:1-21 ☐
97	11:1-22 ☐	11:23-45 ☐	12:1-13 ☐	Hosea 1:1-11 ☐	2:1-23 ☐	3:1—4:19 ☐	5:1-15 ☐
98	6:1-11 ☐	7:1-16 ☐	8:1-14 ☐	9:1-17 ☐	10:1-15 ☐	11:1-12 ☐	12:1-14 ☐
99	13:1—14:9 ☐	Joel 1:1-20 ☐	2:1-16 ☐	2:17-32 ☐	3:1-21 ☐	Amos 1:1-15 ☐	2:1-16 ☐
100	3:1-15 ☐	4:1—5:27 ☐	6:1—7:17 ☐	8:1—9:15 ☐	Obad. 1-21 ☐	Jonah 1:1-17 ☐	2:1—4:11 ☐
101	Micah 1:1-16 ☐	2:1—3:12 ☐	4:1—5:15 ☐	6:1—7:20 ☐	Nahum 1:1-15 ☐	2:1—3:19 ☐	Hab. 1:1-17 ☐
102	2:1-20 ☐	3:1-19 ☐	Zeph. 1:1-18 ☐	2:1-15 ☐	3:1-20 ☐	Hag. 1:1-15 ☐	2:1-23 ☐
103	Zech. 1:1-21 ☐	2:1-13 ☐	3:1-10 ☐	4:1-14 ☐	5:1—6:15 ☐	7:1—8:23 ☐	9:1-17 ☐
104	10:1—11:17 ☐	12:1—13:9 ☐	14:1-21 ☐	Mal. 1:1-14 ☐	2:1-17 ☐	3:1-18 ☐	4:1-6 ☐

Reading Schedule for the Recovery Version of the New Testament with Footnotes

Wk.	Lord's Day	Monday	Tuesday	Wednesday	Thursday	Friday	Saturday
1	Matt. 1:1-2 ☐	1:3-7 ☐	1:8-17 ☐	1:18-25 ☐	2:1-23 ☐	3:1-6 ☐	3:7-17 ☐
2	4:1-11 ☐	4:12-25 ☐	5:1-4 ☐	5:5-12 ☐	5:13-20 ☐	5:21-26 ☐	5:27-48 ☐
3	6:1-8 ☐	6:9-18 ☐	6:19-34 ☐	7:1-12 ☐	7:13-29 ☐	8:1-13 ☐	8:14-22 ☐
4	8:23-34 ☐	9:1-13 ☐	9:14-17 ☐	9:18-34 ☐	9:35—10:5 ☐	10:6-25 ☐	10:26-42 ☐
5	11:1-15 ☐	11:16-30 ☐	12:1-14 ☐	12:15-32 ☐	12:33-42 ☐	12:43—13:2 ☐	13:3-12 ☐
6	13:13-30 ☐	13:31-43 ☐	13:44-58 ☐	14:1-13 ☐	14:14-21 ☐	14:22-36 ☐	15:1-20 ☐
7	15:21-31 ☐	15:32-39 ☐	16:1-12 ☐	16:13-20 ☐	16:21-28 ☐	17:1-13 ☐	17:14-27 ☐
8	18:1-14 ☐	18:15-22 ☐	18:23-35 ☐	19:1-15 ☐	19:16-30 ☐	20:1-16 ☐	20:17-34 ☐
9	21:1-11 ☐	21:12-22 ☐	21:23-32 ☐	21:33-46 ☐	22:1-22 ☐	22:23-33 ☐	22:34-46 ☐
10	23:1-12 ☐	23:13-39 ☐	24:1-14 ☐	24:15-31 ☐	24:32-51 ☐	25:1-13 ☐	25:14-30 ☐
11	25:31-46 ☐	26:1-16 ☐	26:17-35 ☐	26:36-46 ☐	26:47-64 ☐	26:65-75 ☐	27:1-26 ☐
12	27:27-44 ☐	27:45-56 ☐	27:57—28:15 ☐	28:16-20 ☐	Mark 1:1 ☐	1:2-6 ☐	1:7-13 ☐
13	1:14-28 ☐	1:29-45 ☐	2:1-12 ☐	2:13-28 ☐	3:1-19 ☐	3:20-35 ☐	4:1-25 ☐
14	4:26-41 ☐	5:1-20 ☐	5:21-43 ☐	6:1-29 ☐	6:30-56 ☐	7:1-23 ☐	7:24-37 ☐
15	8:1-26 ☐	8:27—9:1 ☐	9:2-29 ☐	9:30-50 ☐	10:1-16 ☐	10:17-34 ☐	10:35-52 ☐
16	11:1-16 ☐	11:17-33 ☐	12:1-27 ☐	12:28-44 ☐	13:1-13 ☐	13:14-37 ☐	14:1-26 ☐
17	14:27-52 ☐	14:53-72 ☐	15:1-15 ☐	15:16-47 ☐	16:1-8 ☐	16:9-20 ☐	Luke 1:1-4 ☐
18	1:5-25 ☐	1:26-46 ☐	1:47-56 ☐	1:57-80 ☐	2:1-8 ☐	2:9-20 ☐	2:21-39 ☐
19	2:40-52 ☐	3:1-20 ☐	3:21-38 ☐	4:1-13 ☐	4:14-30 ☐	4:31-44 ☐	5:1-26 ☐
20	5:27—6:16 ☐	6:17-38 ☐	6:39-49 ☐	7:1-17 ☐	7:18-23 ☐	7:24-35 ☐	7:36-50 ☐
21	8:1-15 ☐	8:16-25 ☐	8:26-39 ☐	8:40-56 ☐	9:1-17 ☐	9:18-26 ☐	9:27-36 ☐
22	9:37-50 ☐	9:51-62 ☐	10:1-11 ☐	10:12-24 ☐	10:25-37 ☐	10:38-42 ☐	11:1-13 ☐
23	11:14-26 ☐	11:27-36 ☐	11:37-54 ☐	12:1-12 ☐	12:13-21 ☐	12:22-34 ☐	12:35-48 ☐
24	12:49-59 ☐	13:1-9 ☐	13:10-17 ☐	13:18-30 ☐	13:31—14:6 ☐	14:7-14 ☐	14:15-24 ☐
25	14:25-35 ☐	15:1-10 ☐	15:11-21 ☐	15:22-32 ☐	16:1-13 ☐	16:14-22 ☐	16:23-31 ☐
26	17:1-19 ☐	17:20-37 ☐	18:1-14 ☐	18:15-30 ☐	18:31-43 ☐	19:1-10 ☐	19:11-27 ☐

Reading Schedule for the Recovery Version of the New Testament with Footnotes

Wk.	Lord's Day	Monday	Tuesday	Wednesday	Thursday	Friday	Saturday
27	Luke 19:28-48 ☐	20:1-19 ☐	20:20-38 ☐	20:39—21:4 ☐	21:5-27 ☐	21:28-38 ☐	22:1-20 ☐
28	22:21-38 ☐	22:39-54 ☐	22:55-71 ☐	23:1-43 ☐	23:44-56 ☐	24:1-12 ☐	24:13-35 ☐
29	24:36-53 ☐	John 1:1-13 ☐	1:14-18 ☐	1:19-34 ☐	1:35-51 ☐	2:1-11 ☐	2:12-22 ☐
30	2:23—3:13 ☐	3:14-21 ☐	3:22-36 ☐	4:1-14 ☐	4:15-26 ☐	4:27-42 ☐	4:43-54 ☐
31	5:1-16 ☐	5:17-30 ☐	5:31-47 ☐	6:1-15 ☐	6:16-31 ☐	6:32-51 ☐	6:52-71 ☐
32	7:1-9 ☐	7:10-24 ☐	7:25-36 ☐	7:37-52 ☐	7:53—8:11 ☐	8:12-27 ☐	8:28-44 ☐
33	8:45-59 ☐	9:1-13 ☐	9:14-34 ☐	9:35—10:9 ☐	10:10-30 ☐	10:31—11:4 ☐	11:5-22 ☐
34	11:23-40 ☐	11:41-57 ☐	12:1-11 ☐	12:12-24 ☐	12:25-36 ☐	12:37-50 ☐	13:1-11 ☐
35	13:12-30 ☐	13:31-38 ☐	14:1-6 ☐	14:7-20 ☐	14:21-31 ☐	15:1-11 ☐	15:12-27 ☐
36	16:1-15 ☐	16:16-33 ☐	17:1-5 ☐	17:6-13 ☐	17:14-24 ☐	17:25—18:11 ☐	18:12-27 ☐
37	18:28-40 ☐	19:1-16 ☐	19:17-30 ☐	19:31-42 ☐	20:1-13 ☐	20:14-18 ☐	20:19-22 ☐
38	20:23-31 ☐	21:1-14 ☐	21:15-22 ☐	21:23-25 ☐	Acts 1:1-8 ☐	1:9-14 ☐	1:15-26 ☐
39	2:1-13 ☐	2:14-21 ☐	2:22-36 ☐	2:37-41 ☐	2:42-47 ☐	3:1-18 ☐	3:19—4:22 ☐
40	4:23-37 ☐	5:1-16 ☐	5:17-32 ☐	5:33-42 ☐	6:1—7:1 ☐	7:2-29 ☐	7:30-60 ☐
41	8:1-13 ☐	8:14-25 ☐	8:26-40 ☐	9:1-19 ☐	9:20-43 ☐	10:1-16 ☐	10:17-33 ☐
42	10:34-48 ☐	11:1-18 ☐	11:19-30 ☐	12:1-25 ☐	13:1-12 ☐	13:13-43 ☐	13:44—14:5 ☐
43	14:6-28 ☐	15:1-12 ☐	15:13-34 ☐	15:35—16:5 ☐	16:6-18 ☐	16:19-40 ☐	17:1-18 ☐
44	17:19-34 ☐	18:1-17 ☐	18:18-28 ☐	19:1-20 ☐	19:21-41 ☐	20:1-12 ☐	20:13-38 ☐
45	21:1-14 ☐	21:15-26 ☐	21:27-40 ☐	22:1-21 ☐	22:22-29 ☐	22:30—23:11 ☐	23:12-15 ☐
46	23:16-30 ☐	23:31—24:21 ☐	24:22—25:5 ☐	25:6-27 ☐	26:1-13 ☐	26:14-32 ☐	27:1-26 ☐
47	27:27—28:10 ☐	28:11-22 ☐	28:23-31 ☐	Rom. 1:1-2 ☐	1:3-7 ☐	1:8-17 ☐	1:18-25 ☐
48	1:26—2:10 ☐	2:11-29 ☐	3:1-20 ☐	3:21-31 ☐	4:1-12 ☐	4:13-25 ☐	5:1-11 ☐
49	5:12-17 ☐	5:18—6:5 ☐	6:6-11 ☐	6:12-23 ☐	7:1-12 ☐	7:13-25 ☐	8:1-2 ☐
50	8:3-6 ☐	8:7-13 ☐	8:14-25 ☐	8:26-39 ☐	9:1-18 ☐	9:19—10:3 ☐	10:4-15 ☐
51	10:16—11:10 ☐	11:11-22 ☐	11:23-36 ☐	12:1-3 ☐	12:4-21 ☐	13:1-14 ☐	14:1-12 ☐
52	14:13-23 ☐	15:1-13 ☐	15:14-33 ☐	16:1-5 ☐	16:6-24 ☐	16:25-27 ☐	1 Cor. 1:1-4 ☐

Reading Schedule for the Recovery Version of the New Testament with Footnotes

Wk.	Lord's Day	Monday	Tuesday	Wednesday	Thursday	Friday	Saturday
53	1 Cor. 1:5-9 ☐	1:10-17 ☐	1:18-31 ☐	2:1-5 ☐	2:6-10 ☐	2:11-16 ☐	3:1-9 ☐
54	3:10-13 ☐	3:14-23 ☐	4:1-9 ☐	4:10-21 ☐	5:1-13 ☐	6:1-11 ☐	6:12-20 ☐
55	7:1-16 ☐	7:17-24 ☐	7:25-40 ☐	8:1-13 ☐	9:1-15 ☐	9:16-27 ☐	10:1-4 ☐
56	10:5-13 ☐	10:14-33 ☐	11:1-6 ☐	11:7-16 ☐	11:17-26 ☐	11:27-34 ☐	12:1-11 ☐
57	12:12-22 ☐	12:23-31 ☐	13:1-13 ☐	14:1-12 ☐	14:13-25 ☐	14:26-33 ☐	14:34-40 ☐
58	15:1-19 ☐	15:20-28 ☐	15:29-34 ☐	15:35-49 ☐	15:50-58 ☐	16:1-9 ☐	16:10-24 ☐
59	2 Cor. 1:1-4 ☐	1:5-14 ☐	1:15-22 ☐	1:23—2:11 ☐	2:12-17 ☐	3:1-6 ☐	3:7-11 ☐
60	3:12-18 ☐	4:1-6 ☐	4:7-12 ☐	4:13-18 ☐	5:1-8 ☐	5:9-15 ☐	5:16-21 ☐
61	6:1-13 ☐	6:14—7:4 ☐	7:5-16 ☐	8:1-15 ☐	8:16-24 ☐	9:1-15 ☐	10:1-6 ☐
62	10:7-18 ☐	11:1-15 ☐	11:16-33 ☐	12:1-10 ☐	12:11-21 ☐	13:1-10 ☐	13:11-14 ☐
63	Gal. 1:1-5 ☐	1:6-14 ☐	1:15-24 ☐	2:1-13 ☐	2:14-21 ☐	3:1-4 ☐	3:5-14 ☐
64	3:15-22 ☐	3:23-29 ☐	4:1-7 ☐	4:8-20 ☐	4:21-31 ☐	5:1-12 ☐	5:13-21 ☐
65	5:22-26 ☐	6:1-10 ☐	6:11-15 ☐	6:16-18 ☐	Eph. 1:1-3 ☐	1:4-6 ☐	1:7-10 ☐
66	1:11-14 ☐	1:15-18 ☐	1:19-23 ☐	2:1-5 ☐	2:6-10 ☐	2:11-14 ☐	2:15-18 ☐
67	2:19-22 ☐	3:1-7 ☐	3:8-13 ☐	3:14-18 ☐	3:19-21 ☐	4:1-4 ☐	4:5-10 ☐
68	4:11-16 ☐	4:17-24 ☐	4:25-32 ☐	5:1-10 ☐	5:11-21 ☐	5:22-26 ☐	5:27-33 ☐
69	6:1-9 ☐	6:10-14 ☐	6:15-18 ☐	6:19-24 ☐	Phil. 1:1-7 ☐	1:8-18 ☐	1:19-26 ☐
70	1:27—2:4 ☐	2:5-11 ☐	2:12-16 ☐	2:17-30 ☐	3:1-6 ☐	3:7-11 ☐	3:12-16 ☐
71	3:17-21 ☐	4:1-9 ☐	4:10-23 ☐	Col. 1:1-8 ☐	1:9-13 ☐	1:14-23 ☐	1:24-29 ☐
72	2:1-7 ☐	2:8-15 ☐	2:16-23 ☐	3:1-4 ☐	3:5-15 ☐	3:16-25 ☐	4:1-18 ☐
73	1 Thes. 1:1-3 ☐	1:4-10 ☐	2:1-12 ☐	2:13—3:5 ☐	3:6-13 ☐	4:1-10 ☐	4:11—5:11 ☐
74	5:12-28 ☐	2 Thes. 1:1-12 ☐	2:1-17 ☐	3:1-18 ☐	1 Tim. 1:1-2 ☐	1:3-4 ☐	1:5-14 ☐
75	1:15-20 ☐	2:1-7 ☐	2:8-15 ☐	3:1-13 ☐	3:14—4:5 ☐	4:6-16 ☐	5:1-25 ☐
76	6:1-10 ☐	6:11-21 ☐	2 Tim. 1:1-10 ☐	1:11-18 ☐	2:1-15 ☐	2:16-26 ☐	3:1-13 ☐
77	3:14—4:8 ☐	4:9-22 ☐	Titus 1:1-4 ☐	1:5-16 ☐	2:1-15 ☐	3:1-8 ☐	3:9-15 ☐
78	Philem. 1:1-11 ☐	1:12-25 ☐	Heb. 1:1-2 ☐	1:3-5 ☐	1:6-14 ☐	2:1-9 ☐	2:10-18 ☐

Reading Schedule for the Recovery Version of the New Testament with Footnotes

Wk.	Lord's Day	Monday	Tuesday	Wednesday	Thursday	Friday	Saturday
79	Heb. 3:1-6 ☐	3:7-19 ☐	4:1-9 ☐	4:10-13 ☐	4 14-16 ☐	5:1-10 ☐	5:11—6:3 ☐
80	6:4-8 ☐	6:9-20 ☐	7:1-10 ☐	7:11-28 ☐	8:1-6 ☐	8:7-13 ☐	9:1-4 ☐
81	9:5-14 ☐	9:15-28 ☐	10:1-18 ☐	10:19-28 ☐	10:29-39 ☐	11:1-6 ☐	11:7-19 ☐
82	11:20-31 ☐	11:32-40 ☐	12:1-2 ☐	12:3-13 ☐	12:14-17 ☐	12:18-26 ☐	12:27-29 ☐
83	13:1-7 ☐	13:8-12 ☐	13:13-15 ☐	13:16-25 ☐	James 1:1-8 ☐	1:9-18 ☐	1:19-27 ☐
84	2:1-13 ☐	2:14-26 ☐	3:1-18 ☐	4:1-10 ☐	4:11-17 ☐	5:1-12 ☐	5:13-20 ☐
85	1 Pet. 1:1-2 ☐	1:3-4 ☐	1:5 ☐	1:6-9 ☐	1:10-12 ☐	1:13-17 ☐	1:18-25 ☐
86	2:1-3 ☐	2:4-8 ☐	2:9-17 ☐	2:18-25 ☐	3:1-13 ☐	3:14-22 ☐	4:1-6 ☐
87	4:7-16 ☐	4:17-19 ☐	5:1-4 ☐	5:5-9 ☐	5:10-14 ☐	2 Pet. 1:1-2 ☐	1:3-4 ☐
88	1:5-8 ☐	1:9-11 ☐	1:12-18 ☐	1:19-21 ☐	2:1-3 ☐	2:4-11 ☐	2:12-22 ☐
89	3:1-6 ☐	3:7-9 ☐	3:10-12 ☐	3:13-15 ☐	3:16 ☐	3:17-18 ☐	1 John 1:1-2 ☐
90	1:3-4 ☐	1:5 ☐	1:6 ☐	1:7 ☐	1:8-10 ☐	2:1-2 ☐	2:3-11 ☐
91	2:12-14 ☐	2:15-19 ☐	2:20-23 ☐	2:24-27 ☐	2:28-29 ☐	3:1-5 ☐	3:6-10 ☐
92	3:11-18 ☐	3:19-24 ☐	4:1-6 ☐	4:7-11 ☐	4:12-15 ☐	4:16—5:3 ☐	5:4-13 ☐
93	5:14-17 ☐	5:18-21 ☐	2 John 1:1-3 ☐	1:4-9 ☐	1:10-13 ☐	3 John 1:1-6 ☐	1:7-14 ☐
94	Jude 1:1-4 ☐	1:5-10 ☐	1:11-19 ☐	1:20-25 ☐	Rev. 1:1-3 ☐	1:4-6 ☐	1:7-11 ☐
95	1:12-13 ☐	1:14-16 ☐	1:17-20 ☐	2:1-6 ☐	2:7 ☐	2:8-9 ☐	2:10-11 ☐
96	2:12-14 ☐	2:15-17 ☐	2:18-23 ☐	2:24-29 ☐	3:1-3 ☐	3:4-6 ☐	3:7-9 ☐
97	3:10-13 ☐	3:14-18 ☐	3:19-22 ☐	4:1-5 ☐	4:5-7 ☐	4:8-11 ☐	5:1-6 ☐
98	5:7-14 ☐	6:1-8 ☐	6:9-17 ☐	7:1-8 ☐	7:9-17 ☐	8:1-6 ☐	8:7-12 ☐
99	8:13—9:11 ☐	9:12-21 ☐	10:1-4 ☐	10:5-11 ☐	11:1-4 ☐	11:5-14 ☐	11:15-19 ☐
100	12:1-4 ☐	12:5-9 ☐	12:10-18 ☐	13:1-10 ☐	13:11-18 ☐	14:1-5 ☐	14:6-12 ☐
101	14:13-20 ☐	15:1-8 ☐	16:1-12 ☐	16:13-21 ☐	17:1-6 ☐	17:7-18 ☐	18:1-8 ☐
102	18:9—19:4 ☐	19:5-10 ☐	19:11-16 ☐	19:17-21 ☐	20:1-6 ☐	20:7-10 ☐	20:11-15 ☐
103	21:1 ☐	21:2 ☐	21:3-8 ☐	21:9-13 ☐	21:14-18 ☐	21:19-21 ☐	21:22-27 ☐
104	22:1 ☐	22:2 ☐	22:3-11 ☐	22:12-15 ☐	22:16-17 ☐	22:18-21 ☐	

Week 1 — Day 6 — Today's verses

Eph. 3:17 That Christ may make His home in your hearts through faith, that you, being rooted and grounded in love.

21 To Him be the glory in the church and in Christ Jesus unto all the generations forever and ever. Amen.

_____
Date

Week 1 — Day 5 — Today's verses

2 Cor. 4:16 Therefore we do not lose heart; but though our outer man is decaying, yet our inner *man* is being renewed day by day.

5:15 And He died for all that those who live may no longer live to themselves but to Him who died for them and has been raised.

_____
Date

Week 1 — Day 4 — Today's verses

Gal. 2:20 I am crucified with Christ; and *it is* no longer I *who* live, but *it is* Christ *who* lives in me; and the *life* which I now live in the flesh I live in faith, the *faith* of the Son of God, who loved me and gave Himself up for me.

Col. 3:4 When Christ our life is manifested, then you also will be manifested with Him in glory.

_____
Date

Week 1 — Day 3 — Today's verses

John 14:23 Jesus answered and said to him, If anyone loves Me, he will keep My word, and My Father will love him, and We will come to him and make an abode with him.

Col. 3:11 Where there cannot be Greek and Jew, circumcision and uncircumcision, barbarian, Scythian, slave, free man, but Christ is all and in all.

_____
Date

Week 1 — Day 2 — Today's verses

Eph. 2:10 For we are His masterpiece, created in Christ Jesus for good works, which God prepared beforehand in order that we would walk in them.

2 Tim. 2:21 If therefore anyone cleanses himself from these, he will be a vessel unto honor, sanctified, useful to the master, prepared unto every good work.

_____
Date

Week 1 — Day 1 — Today's verses

Phil. 2:13 For it is God who operates in you both the willing and the working for *His* good pleasure.

Gal. 4:19 My children, with whom I travail again in birth until Christ is formed in you.

_____
Date

Week 2 — Day 6

Gen. 49:21   Naphtali is a hind let loose; he gives beautiful words.

Hab. 3:19   Jehovah the Lord is my strength; and He makes my feet like hinds' *feet* and will cause me to walk on my high places....

_____
Date

Week 2 — Day 5

Eph. 4:11-12   And He Himself gave some as apostles and some as prophets and some as evangelists and some as shepherds and teachers, for the perfecting of the saints unto the work of the ministry, unto the building up of the Body of Christ.

_____
Date

Week 2 — Day 4

Matt. 16:24   Then Jesus said to His disciples, If anyone wants to come after Me, let him deny himself and take up his cross and follow Me.

S. S. 2:1-2   I am a rose of Sharon, a lily of the valleys. As a lily among thorns, so is my love among the daughters.

_____
Date

Week 2 — Day 3

Gal. 2:20   I am crucified with Christ; and *it is* no longer I *who* live, but *it is* Christ *who* lives in me; and the *life* which I now live in the flesh I live in faith, the *faith* of the Son of God, who loved me and gave Himself up for me.

1 Cor. 15:10   But by the grace of God I am what I am; and His grace unto me did not turn out to be in vain, but, on the contrary, I labored more abundantly than all of them, yet not I but the grace of God which is with me.

_____
Date

Week 2 — Day 2

Rom. 12:2   And do not be fashioned according to this age, but be transformed by the renewing of the mind that you may prove what the will of God is, that which is good and well pleasing and perfect.

1 Tim. 3:15   But if I delay, *I write* that you may know how one ought to conduct himself in the house of God, which is the church of the living God, the pillar and base of the truth.

_____
Date

Week 2 — Day 1

Gen. 28:18   And Jacob rose up early in the morning and took the stone that he had put under his head, and he set it up as a pillar and poured oil on top of it.

Rev. 3:12   He who overcomes, him I will make a pillar in the temple of My God, and he shall by no means go out anymore, and I will write upon him the name of My God and the name of the city of My God, the New Jerusalem,...and My new name.

_____
Date

Week 3 — Day 4 — Today's verses

Rom. Because the mind set on the flesh is enmity
8:7-9 against God; for it is not subject to the law of
God, for neither can it be. And those who are
in the flesh cannot please God. But you are
not in the flesh, but in the spirit, if indeed the
Spirit of God dwells in you. Yet if anyone does
not have the Spirit of Christ, he is not of Him.

_____
Date

Week 3 — Day 5 — Today's verses

1 Cor. Therefore I make known to you that no
12:3 one speaking in the Spirit of God says, Jesus *is* accursed; and no one can say, Jesus
is Lord! except in the Holy Spirit.

1 Thes. Unceasingly pray.
5:17

_____
Date

Week 3 — Day 6 — Today's verses

Rom. That the righteous requirement of the law
8:4 might be fulfilled in us, who do not walk
according to the flesh but according to
the spirit.

12:4-5 For just as in one body we have many
members, and all the members do not
have the same function, so we who are
many are one Body in Christ, and individually members one of another.

_____
Date

Week 3 — Day 1 — Today's verses

Gal. I am crucified with Christ; and *it is* no
2:20 longer I *who* live, but *it is* Christ *who* lives
in me; and the *life* which I now live in the
flesh I live in faith, the *faith* of the Son of
God, who loved me and gave Himself up
for me.

Phil. For to me, to live is Christ and to die is
1:21 gain.

_____
Date

Week 3 — Day 2 — Today's verses

John As the living Father has sent Me and I live
6:57 because of the Father, so he who eats Me,
he also shall live because of Me.

14:19 Yet a little while and the world beholds
Me no longer, but you behold Me; because I live, you also shall live.

_____
Date

Week 3 — Day 3 — Today's verses

Rom. That the righteous requirement of the law
8:4-6 might be fulfilled in us, who do not walk
according to the flesh but according to the
spirit. For those who are according to the
flesh mind the things of the flesh; but those
who are according to the spirit, the things
of the Spirit. For the mind set on the flesh is
death, but the mind set on the spirit is life
and peace.

_____
Date

Week 4 — Day 4   Today's verses

John   Jesus answered, Truly, truly, I say to you,
3:5-6   Unless one is born of water and the Spirit,
         he cannot enter into the kingdom of God.
         That which is born of the flesh is flesh, and
         that which is born of the Spirit is spirit.

2 Cor.   And having the same spirit of faith ac-
4:13   cording to that which is written, "I be-
         lieved, therefore I spoke," we also believe,
         therefore we also speak.

Date

Week 4 — Day 5   Today's verses

Matt.   Blessed are the pure in heart, for they
5:8   shall see God.

3   Blessed are the poor in spirit, for theirs is
         the kingdom of the heavens.

Eph.   That He would grant you...to be strength-
3:16-17 ened with power through His Spirit into
         the inner man, that Christ may make His
         home in your hearts through faith...

Date

Week 4 — Day 6   Today's verses

Eph.   But to Him who is able to do superabun-
3:20-21 dantly above all that we ask or think, ac-
         cording to the power which operates in
         us, to Him be the glory in the church and
         in Christ Jesus unto all the generations for-
         ever and ever. Amen.

Date

Week 4 — Day 1   Today's verses

Ezek.   I will also give you a new heart, and a new
36:26-27 spirit I will put within you; and I will take
         away the heart of stone out of your flesh,
         and I will give you a heart of flesh. And I
         will put My Spirit within you and cause
         you to walk in My statutes, and My ordi-
         nances you shall keep and do.

Date

Week 4 — Day 2   Today's verses

2 Cor.   Our mouth is opened to you, Corinthians;
6:11-13 our heart is enlarged. You are not con-
         stricted in us, but you are constricted in
         your inward parts. But for a recompense
         in kind, I speak as to children, you also be
         enlarged.

Psa.   I run the way of Your commandments, for
119:32   You enlarge my heart.

Date

Week 4 — Day 3   Today's verses

Matt.   For if you forgive men their offenses, your
6:14-15 heavenly Father will forgive you also; but
         if you do not forgive men their offenses,
         neither will your Father forgive your offenses.

Date

Week 5 — Day 4   Today's verses

Eph. And walk in love, even as Christ also
5:2 loved us and gave Himself up for us, an offering and a sacrifice to God for a sweet-smelling savor.

1 John And we know and have believed the love
4:16 which God has in us. God is love, and he who abides in love abides in God and God abides in him.

_____
Date

Week 5 — Day 5   Today's verses

Eph. And to know the knowledge-surpassing
3:19 love of Christ, that you may be filled unto all the fullness of God.

4:16 Out from whom all the Body, being joined together and being knit together through every joint of the rich supply and *through* the operation in the measure of each one part, causes the growth of the Body unto the building up of itself in love.

_____
Date

Week 5 — Day 6   Today's verses

1 John But if we walk in the light as He is in the
1:7 light, we have fellowship with one another, and the blood of Jesus His Son cleanses us from every sin.

Eph. For you were once darkness but are now
5:8-9 light in the Lord; walk as children of light (for the fruit of the light *consists* in all goodness and righteousness and truth).

_____
Date

Week 5 — Day 1   Today's verses

Mark "And you shall love the Lord your God
12:30 from your whole heart and from your whole soul and from your whole mind and from your whole strength."

1 Cor. But as it is written, "Things which eye has
2:9 not seen and ear has not heard and *which* have not come up in man's heart; things which God has prepared for those who love Him."

_____
Date

Week 5 — Day 2   Today's verses

2 Tim. Henceforth there is laid up for me the
4:8 crown of righteousness, with which the Lord, the righteous Judge, will recompense me in that day, and not only me but also all those who have loved His appearing.

Eph. Grace be with all those who love our Lord
6:24 Jesus Christ in incorruptibility.

_____
Date

Week 5 — Day 3   Today's verses

John But as many as received Him, to them He
1:12 gave the authority to become children of God, to those who believe into His name.

2 Pet. Through which He has granted to us pre-
1:4 cious and exceedingly great promises that through these you might become partakers of the divine nature, having escaped the corruption which is in the world by lust.

_____
Date

Week 6 — Day 4   **Today's verses**

Matt. And seeing the crowds, He was moved
9:36 with compassion for them, because they
were harassed and cast away like sheep
not having a shepherd.

Luke And he rose up and came to his own fa-
15:20 ther. But while he was still a long way off,
his father saw him and was moved with
compassion, and he ran and fell on his
neck and kissed him affectionately.

_____
Date

Week 6 — Day 5   **Today's verses**

Heb. Now the God of peace, He who brought
13:20 up from the dead our Lord Jesus, the great
Shepherd of the sheep, in the blood of an
eternal covenant.

Rev. And in the midst of the lampstands One like
1:13 the Son of Man, clothed with a garment
reaching to the feet, and girded about at the
breasts with a golden girdle.

_____
Date

Week 6 — Day 6   **Today's verses**

1 Thes. But we were gentle in your midst, as a
2:7 nursing mother would cherish her own
children.

11 Just as you know how we were to each
one of you, as a father to his own children,
exhorting you and consoling *you* and
testifying.

_____
Date

Week 6 — Day 1   **Today's verses**

John ...Jesus said to Simon Peter,...Do you love
21:15-17 Me...? He said to Him, Yes, Lord, You know
that I love You. He said to him, Feed My
lambs. He said to him again a second
time,...Do you love Me? He said to Him,
Yes, Lord, You know that I love You. He said
to him, Shepherd My sheep. He said to him
the third time,...Do you love Me?...And he
said to Him, Lord,...You know that I love
You. Jesus said to him, Feed My sheep.

_____
Date

Week 6 — Day 2   **Today's verses**

1 Pet. Therefore the elders among you I exhort,
5:1-2 who am a fellow elder and witness of the
sufferings of Christ, who am also a partake-
of the glory to be revealed: Shepherd the
flock of God among you, overseeing not
under compulsion but willingly, according
to God; not by seeking gain through base
means but eagerly.

_____
Date

Week 6 — Day 3   **Today's verses**

1 Pet. Nor as lording it over your allotments but
5:3 by becoming patterns of the flock.

John I am the good Shepherd; the good Shep-
10:11 herd lays down His life for the sheep.

_____
Date

Week 7 — Day 4   **Today's verses**

Eph. For which I am an ambassador in a chain,
6:20 that in it I would speak boldly, as I ought
to speak.

Matt. And Jesus came and spoke to them, say-
28:18-19 ing, All authority has been given to Me in
heaven and on earth. Go therefore and
disciple all the nations, baptizing them
into the name of the Father and of the Son
and of the Holy Spirit.

_____
Date

Week 7 — Day 5   **Today's verses**

2 Cor. For our boasting is this, the testimony of
1:12 our conscience, that in singleness and
sincerity of God....in the grace of God,
we have conducted ourselves in the world,
and more abundantly toward you.

2:10 But whom you forgive anything, I also *forgive;* for also what I have forgiven, if I have
forgiven anything, *it is* for your sake in the
person of Christ.

_____
Date

Week 7 — Day 6   **Today's verses**

Matt. But the centurion answered and said,
8:8-9 Lord. I am not fit for You to enter under my
roof; but only speak a word, and my servant will be healed. For I also am a man
under authority, having soldiers under me.
And I say to this one, Go, and he goes; and
to another, Come, and he comes; and to
my slave, Do this, and he does *it.*

_____
Date

Week 7 — Day 1   **Today's verses**

2 Cor. But all things are out from God, who has rec-
5:18-20 onciled us to Himself through Christ and has
given to us the ministry of reconciliation;
namely, that God in Christ was reconciling
the world to Himself, not accounting their
offenses to them, and has put in us the word
of reconciliation. On behalf of Christ then
we are ambassadors, as God entreats *you*
through us; we beseech *you* on behalf of
Christ, Be reconciled to God.

_____
Date

Week 7 — Day 2   **Today's verses**

2 Cor. For the love of Christ constrains us be-
5:14-15 cause we have judged this, that One died
for all, therefore all died; and He died for
all that those who live may no longer live
to themselves but to Him who died for
them and has been raised.

_____
Date

Week 7 — Day 3   **Today's verses**

2 Cor. Our mouth is opened to you, Corinthians;
6:11-13 our heart is enlarged. You are not constricted in us, but you are constricted in
your inward parts. But for a recompense
in kind, I speak as to children, you also be
enlarged.

_____
Date

Week 8 — Day 4	Today's verses
Gal. 1:15-16	But when it pleased God, who set me apart from my mother's womb and called me through His grace, to reveal His Son in me that I might announce Him as the gospel among the Gentiles, immediately I did not confer with flesh and blood.

Date

Week 8 — Day 5	Today's verses
Eph. 3:16-18	That He would grant you, according to the riches of His glory, to be strengthened with power through His Spirit into the inner man, that Christ may make His home in your hearts through faith, that you, being rooted and grounded in love, may be full of strength to apprehend with all the saints what the breadth and length and height and depth are.

Date

Week 8 — Day 6	Today's verses
Eph. 3:19-21	And to know the knowledge-surpassing love of Christ, that you may be filled unto all the fullness of God. But to Him who is able to do superabundantly above all that we ask or think, according to the power which operates in us, to Him be the glory in the church and in Christ Jesus unto all the generations forever and ever. Amen.

Date

Week 8 — Day 1	Today's verses
1 Tim. 3:15	But if I delay, I write that you may know how one ought to conduct himself in the house of God, which is the church of the living God, the pillar and base of the truth.
Eph. 2:14-15	For He Himself is our peace, He who has made both one and has broken down the middle wall of partition,…that He might create the two in Himself into one new man, so making peace.

Date

Week 8 — Day 2	Today's verses
Eph. 2:16	And might reconcile both in one Body to God through the cross, having slain the enmity by it.
Col. 3:10-11	And have put on the new man, which is being renewed unto full knowledge according to the image of Him who created him, where there cannot be Greek and Jew, circumcision and uncircumcision, barbarian, Scythian, slave, free man, but Christ is all and in all.

Date

Week 8 — Day 3	Today's verses
1 Cor. 12:12-13	For even as the body is one and has many members, yet all the members of the body, being many, are one body, so also is the Christ. For also in one Spirit we were all baptized into one Body, whether Jews or Greeks, whether slaves or free, and were all given to drink one Spirit.

Date

The word becomes shining in our being through the divine light. We are constituted w/ Christ as the truth.
Ephesians 2 - the masterpiece of God. This masterpiece is the mingling of God and man - the church, the Body of Christ. Ephesians 2:15 - ordinances divide us. He got rid of every ordinance. He is the sphere and the constituent of the one new man. Christ is all and in all. Only Christ can be in the one new man. Corporately, we all have to take Christ as our person. Eph 4:22 - 25 He wants to dwell in our heart. Eph 3:16, v. 21 the glory is being brought back to Christ. Christ wants to work Himself into our being. We need both truth and life. The growth is out from the Head and into the Head. Life is the inward substance and God is light expressed.

The corporate _____ warrior fulfills Eph. 1:2a. The divine trinity highlights the fact that God's triune divine dispensing has 2 aspects - objective and subjective.

1 John 2:a
Ephesians 6:19-20